I0541464

Trash Poems

Alex Z. Salinas

Trash Poems

© Copyright 2023 by Alex Z. Salinas

All rights reserved. No part of this book can be reproduced in any form by any means without written permission. Please address inquiries to the publisher:

Gnashing Teeth Publishing
242 E Main St
Norman AR 71960

Cover Photography: Karen Cline-Tardiff

Author Photo: Karl Switzer

The cover font is: Apparat and Ubuntu

The interior font is: Times New Roman

Printed in the United States of America.

ISBN: 979-8-9875694-2-9

A Gnashing Teeth Publishing First Edition

words that get in your teeth

Praise for *Trash Poems*

Do not be fooled by the playful nature of these poems! Each one is a tiny bomb packed with broken glass and coffee grounds. Profound and profane, mundane and holy, penned on the detritus of modern urban life, Salinas' *Trash Poems* are anything but disposable—they will stay with you for a long, long time.

—E. D. Watson, author of *Anorexorcism*

One man's trash is
Another scribe's literature—
True & untrue—
   —Receipt poem No. 2

& so as if the poems eased their way into existence onto the page in his most recent collection *Trash Poems*, Alex Z. Salinas deconstructs in a crisp concise language relaxed & urbane segueing between life & modern American lit what constitutes *trash* down to its essence written on gum wrappers, coffee cups, napkins any article not nailed or tied to the ground bits of paper doomed to the recycling bin (there's no fencing Salinas in) become the locus of these fast-paced slipstreamed lyrics that dash & dart across your field of vision leaving you unsure if you want to cross the page at the speed of touch only to get crushed head-on or sideswiped by these delightful insightful verbal sonics along with 150 or so photographs documenting how these poems got writ in the first place this colloquial fluid conversation with the world family friends living & dead this dialogue with the reader & the poet himself unfettered poetry filtered thru the audial lens of the poet's audacious verve in a voice that sings yet stings—image after image—evoke contemporary & classical connections which are yours to make in punchy "sparse lines that spare no spar" to quote another poet as you rummage thru the trash looking for the one item the one gem gum gave up its wrapper for—to salvage—finally to realize you've discovered or uncovered a cache a hoard to plunder—suddenly like a kid in a candy store or a pirate of the Caribbean a lá Captain Jack Sparrow, you've GOT to have them—one man's trash after all—well you just got to dig in

—Fernando Esteban Flores, author of
Ragged Borders, Red Accordion Blues
and *BloodSongs*

How ecstatic (and envious!) I am reading *Trash Poems*. Alex Z. Salinas has manifested a masterpiece of meditative poesy—one part eco/urban art book, one part ADD *Leaves of Grass,* all parts adhering to the Beat's first thought/best thought. From macro ruminations on family and mortality down to micro observations of a BIC pen, a persistent gnat, a looping Kanye video, Salinas takes note of impermanence with a haiku master's eye/mind, dashing it down on the lost and found objects around us: receipts, cups, wrappers, napkins. All of it, trash. *How easily these words can be ash*—a nugget left buried for us within a pithy political poem. But no worries, gentle reader, this book will be there for you when you need it. These messages-not-in-bottles, scooped up and cataloged for our convenience. And all of us, lucky enough to be floating here right now to receive them.

—Harold Whit Williams, author of
A Rain Ancestral and guitarist for
Cotton Mather

Table of Contents

Foreword

I followed along on social media as Alex began posting his "gum wrapper poems." Soon, he started posting more trash with poetry inscribed on it. This wasn't him laboring for days over a poem then transcribing those words onto trash; they were visceral, in-the-moment poems born out of his immediate thoughts and experiences. I was hooked.

I contacted Alex and we finally met for coffee in San Antonio while I was visiting Austin for a few days. We talked about the impact of these poems and what they represented. This wasn't just an experiment in trash and poetry, it was a treatise of what poetry can be. It makes poetry accessible to everyone. It doesn't require a fancy journal, a certain pen, an MFA, a solid grasp of spelling or grammar, or a secluded writing cabin. Poetry can be the note you scribble on the back of a receipt. Poetry can be words in the margins of an AARP magazine. Poetry can be ephemeral, literal trash, words the poet needs to write down—then it can be thrown away. No one has to see what is written.

Mostly, I was thinking about that kid in the back of the class, slouched down in their seat, scowling at being forced to read Dante. Sure, there is a place for Dante; but that kid needs *Trash Poems*. That kid needs to know poetry is a place where they can let out little pieces of themselves where it is safe. Sometimes things just need to be written down. And sometimes thrown away.

Will Alex start a revolution? I hope it's already happening. I hope there is a person who picks up this book and realizes "Hey, I'm a Poet, too!" I hope Alex's poems reach that kid in the back of the class.

Karen Cline-Tardiff
Editor-in-Chief, Gnashing Teeth Publishing

Preface

Several times over, this book shouldn't have existed.

Beginning June 23, 2021, the Original Plan was to jot down poems on a few gum wrappers, post the tiny experiments to social media so that whomever would read them could read them, then toss the trash. Five trash poems became 10, 10 became 20, then the ego took control. "Let's start transcribing this mess onto a Word document," the voice in my head instructed. "Just in case."

In April 2022, I received a message from poet and publisher of Gnashing Teeth Publishing, Karen Cline-Tardiff, inquiring if I was planning to do anything with my stack of trash poems piling up in a Nike shoebox. Shocked and pleased, I responded that nothing was yet planned. In less time than it takes for a cup of coffee to cool, she called dibs on the book for which I was hardly planning.

In March 2023 (months before this publication), Margaret Cavazos, History major and soon-to-be graduate of St. Mary's University, entered the scene with needed optimism as my cataloging intern for course credit. Without Margaret, you wouldn't see the quality of photographs herein that make this book punch up. Without Jennifer Lloyd and Lindsey Passenger Wieck, Ph.D., I wouldn't know Margaret.

Trash Poems was not part of my Original Plan. But here it is.

Of the writing projects I've had the nerve to chip away at, this one has been the most laborious—and I believe it shows beautifully.

On the contrary, the trash poems themselves are ugly. During the course of a year and half in which I answered the call to repurpose each piece chronicled chronologically in this collection, know that I gave it my best shot in the moment and space (physically and mentally) that I was afforded. I captured each of the poems in five minutes' time to an hour and edited none of them subsequently. Pardon the ink rivers of error—such is the punk state of sustained imperfection.

Know that Emily Dickinson penned trash poems in Amherst, Massachusetts, well over a century before it occurred to me in San Antonio, Texas. Know that Mario Santiago Papasquiero, that wandering graphomaniac of Mexico City, poeted on every surface he desired and had the guts to rid the world of his trash verse before his followers had the guts to preserve it wisely.

Know that *Trash Poems* wasn't in my Original Plan, but like poetry itself, maybe that's a lie.

And that's the truth.

Antipoems should be read in the same order in which they were written.

Nicanor Parra

Far as he was concerned, the enemy was lazy

MF DOOM

Present passed
Measured delay
Theoreticals & smelly
 Spray
#1 cause of perfume:
  Death
Spearmint breath / car plumes
Extra gum never hurt anyone!

Gum-wrapper poem (pg. 103)

6/24/21

Cicada shell baking on
Adobe wall
Specter of
Marx's beard
Spread wide on
Mien of
Liver jam / Smucker's brand
Oh man!
Cosmopolitan Foil-Wrap oblivion

Gum-wrapper poem No. 2 (pg. 103)

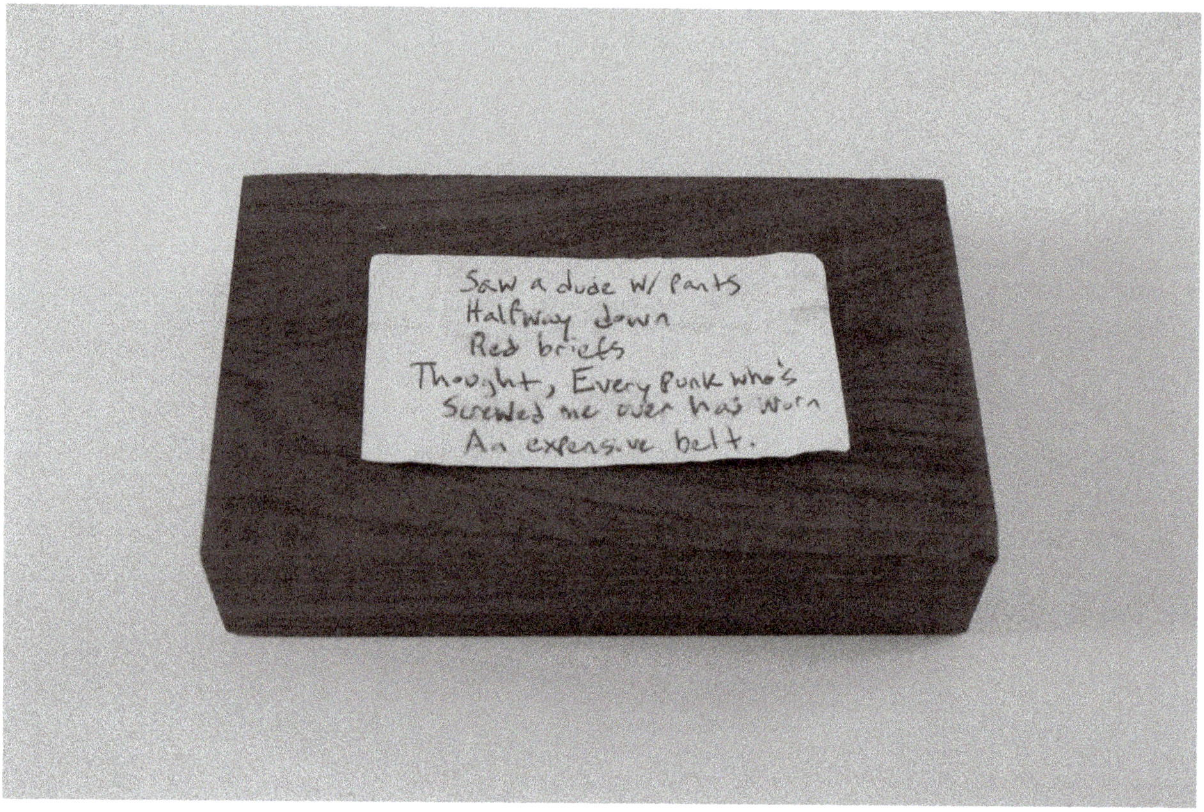

Gum-wrapper poem No. 3 (pg. 104)

Gum-wrapper poem No. 4 (pg. 104)

Red-napkin poem (pg. 105)

Coffee-sleeve poem (pg. 105)

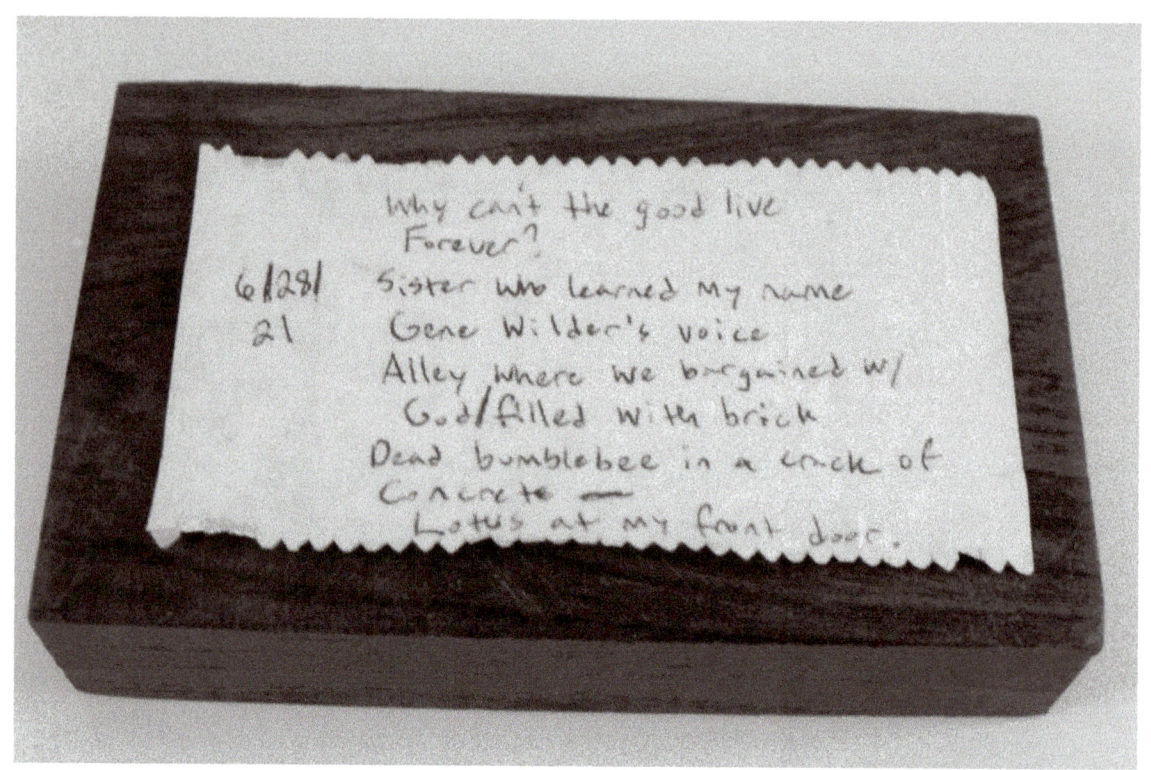

Gum-wrapper poem No. 5 (pg. 106)

Coffee-sleeve poem No. 2 (pg. 106)

Coffe-sleeve poem No. 3 (pg. 107)

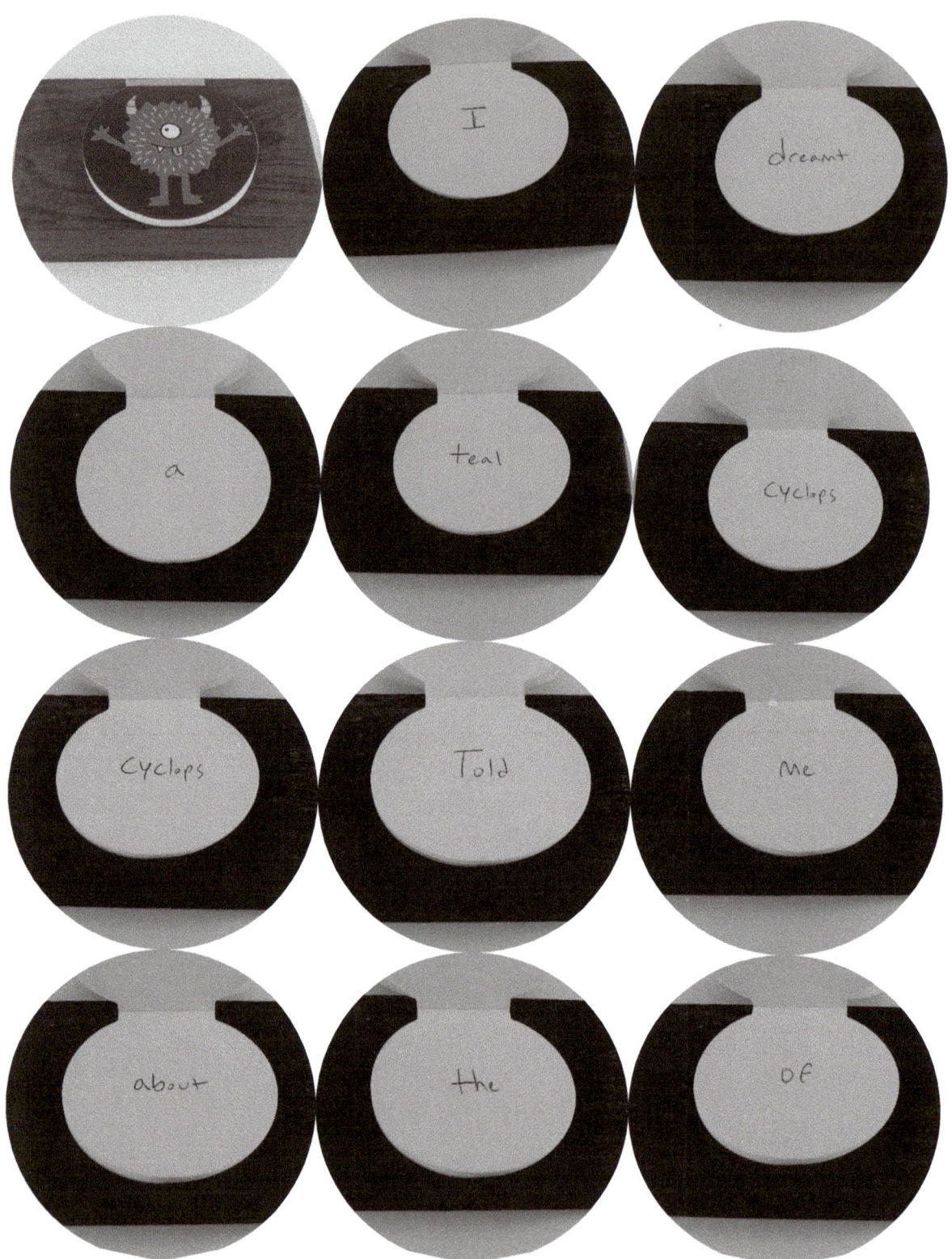

I dreamt a teal Cyclops Cyclops Told Me about the of

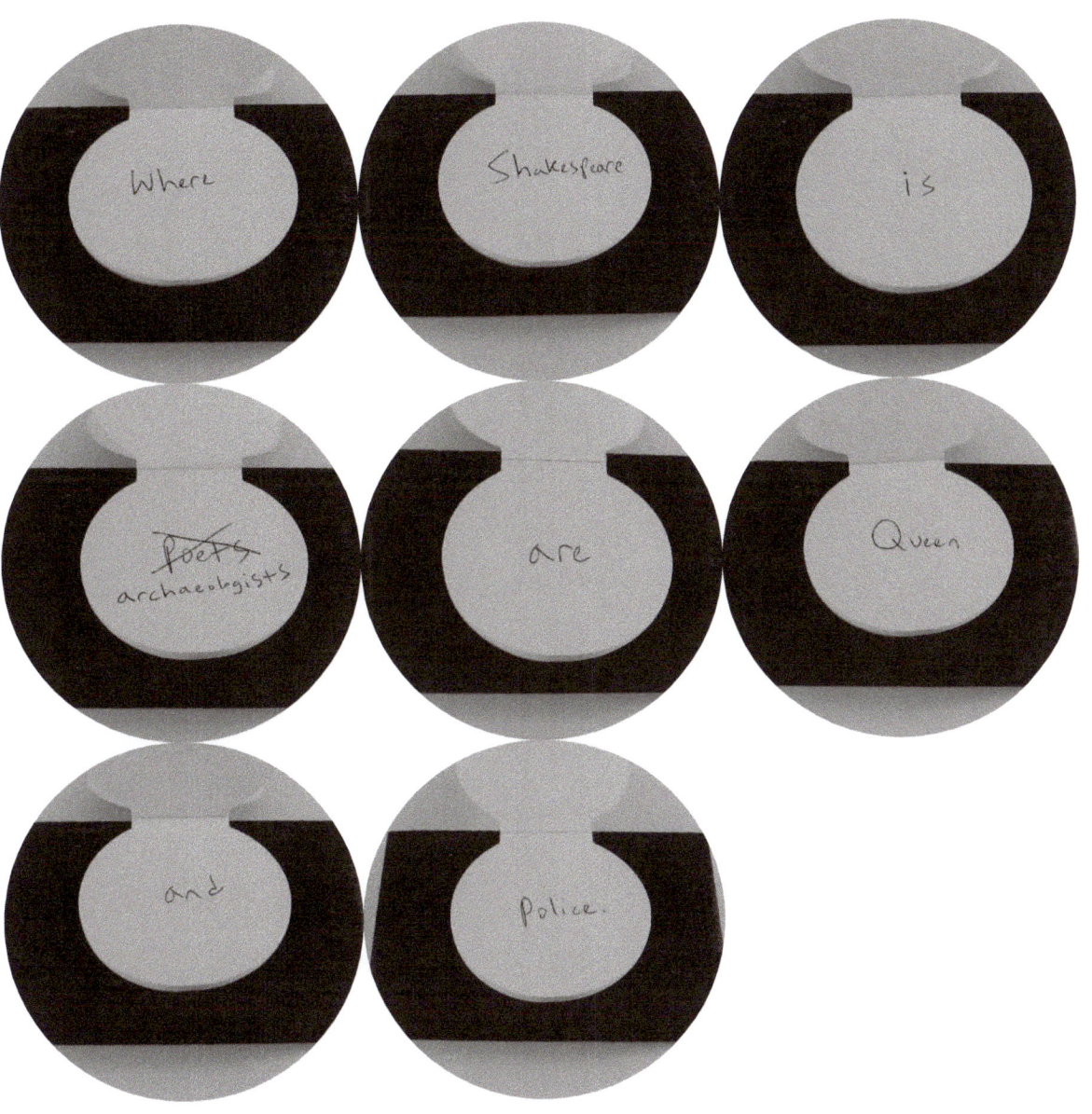

Flip-book poem (pg. 107)

ST·MARYS·UNIVERSITY

My shirt reads:
"Freedom is never free"
And it's true if you
Pry my chest open
Find my mind a time—
Hardened center
Choosing brutal
Poetry against
The Void —
Goodbye, University of
The Underground —
Dangerous discourse
Always felt safe.

7/01/21

Letterhead poem (pg. 108)

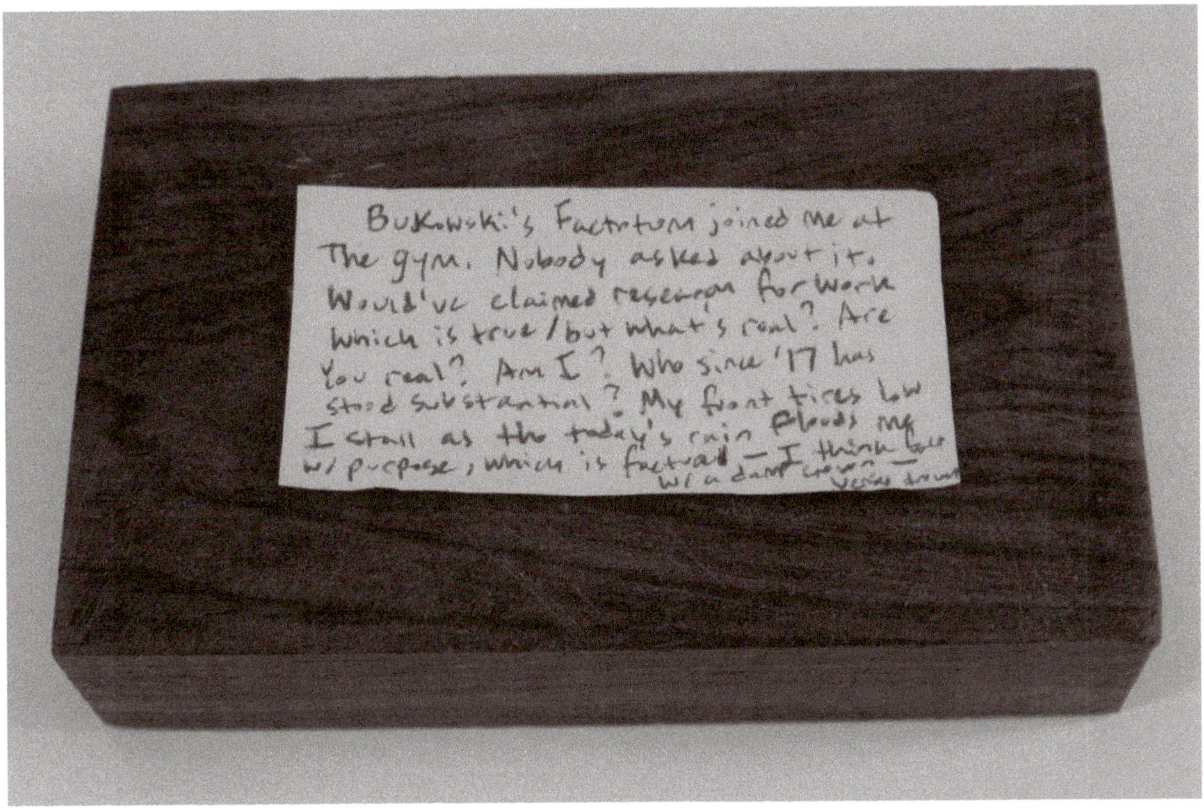

Gum-wrapper poem No. 6 (pg. 108)

Gum-wrapper poem No. 7 (pg. 109)

Gum-wrapper poem No. 8 (pg. 109)

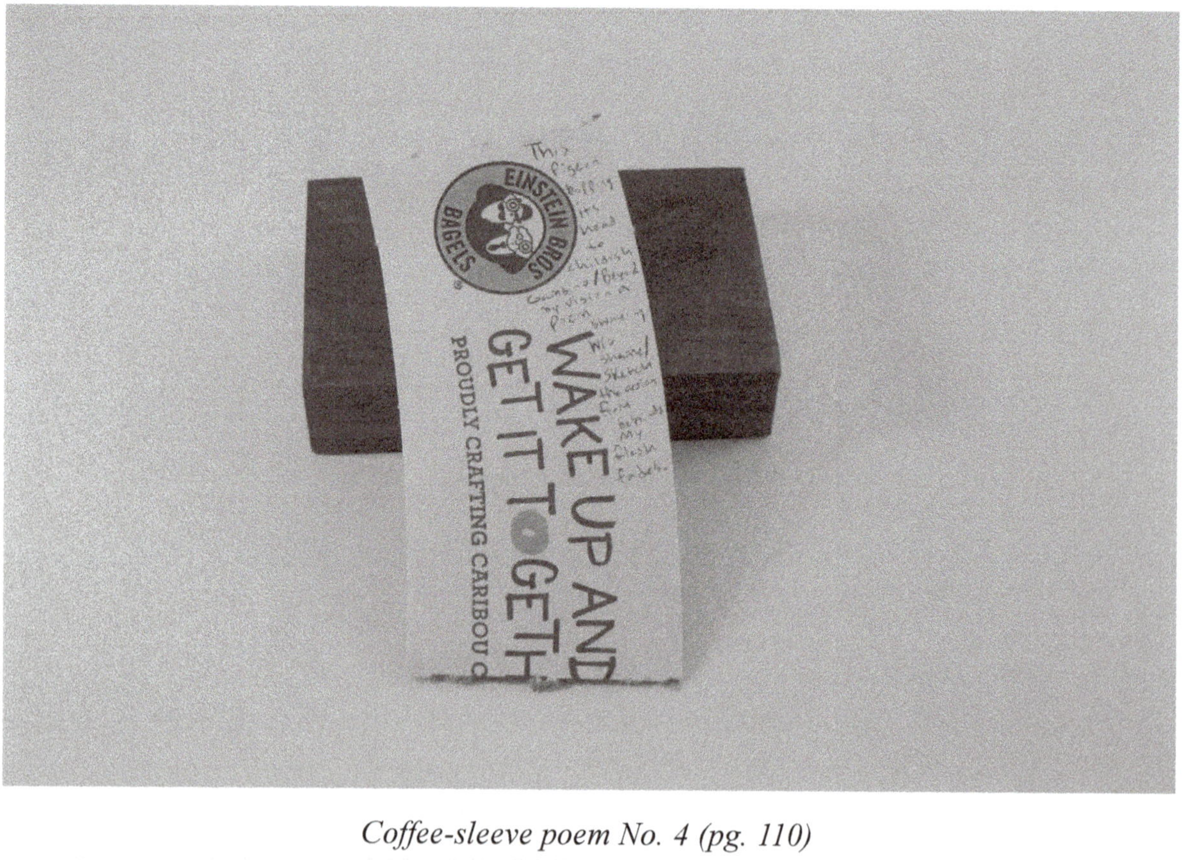

Coffee-sleeve poem No. 4 (pg. 110)

Gun-wrapper peom No. 9 (pg. 110)

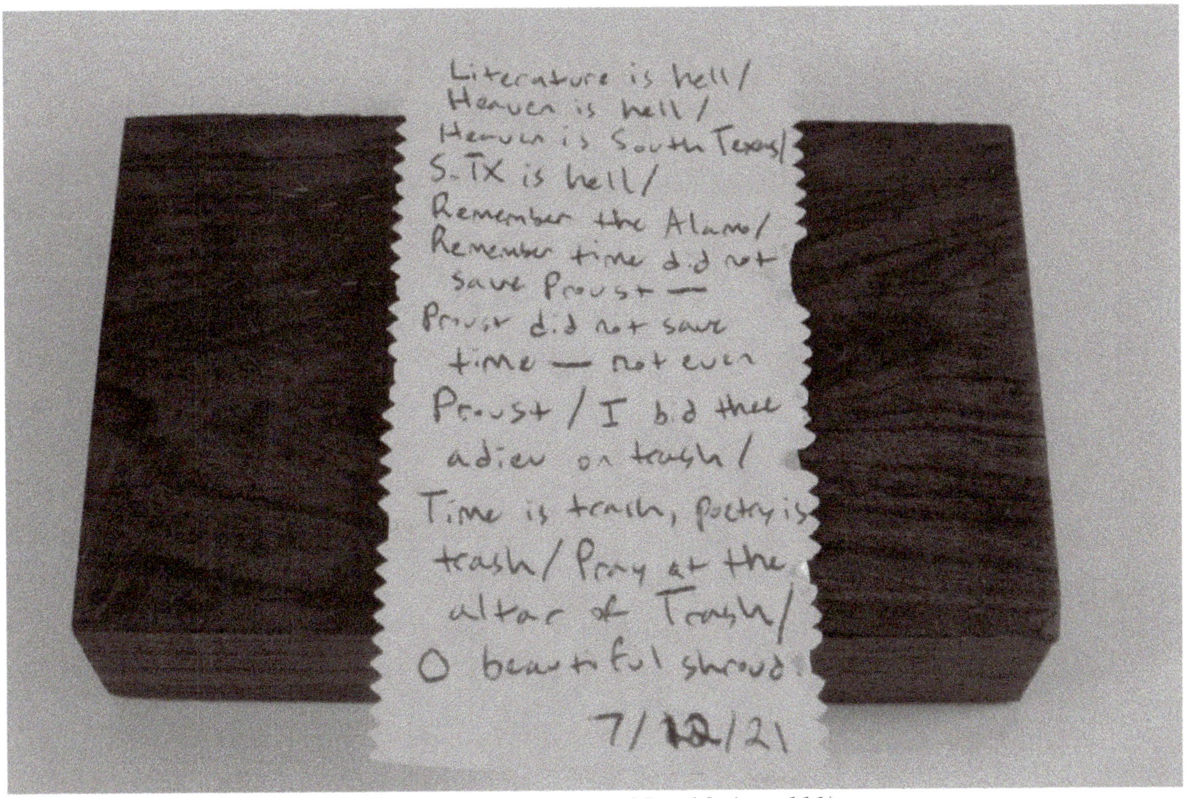

Gum-wrapper poem No. 10 (pg. 111)

Gum-wrapper poem No. 11 (pg. 111)

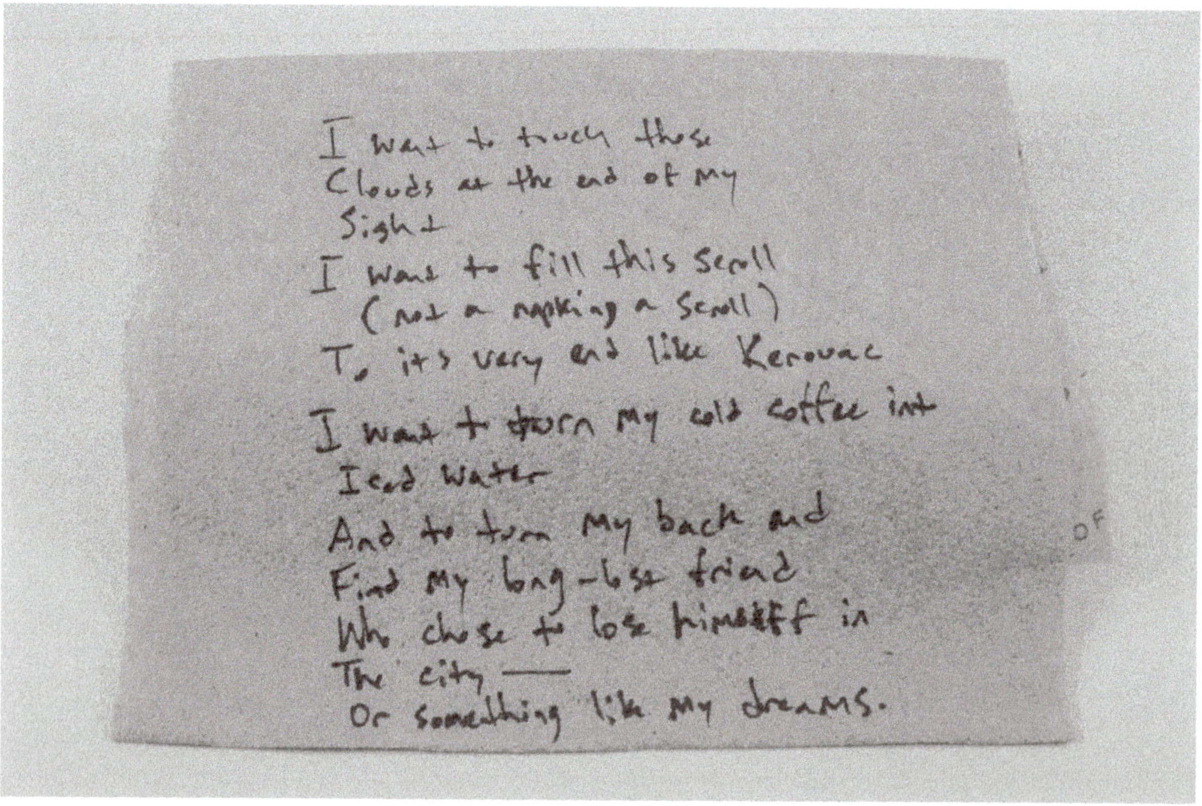

Brown-napkin poem (pg. 112)

Coffee-sleeve poem No. 5 (pg. 112)

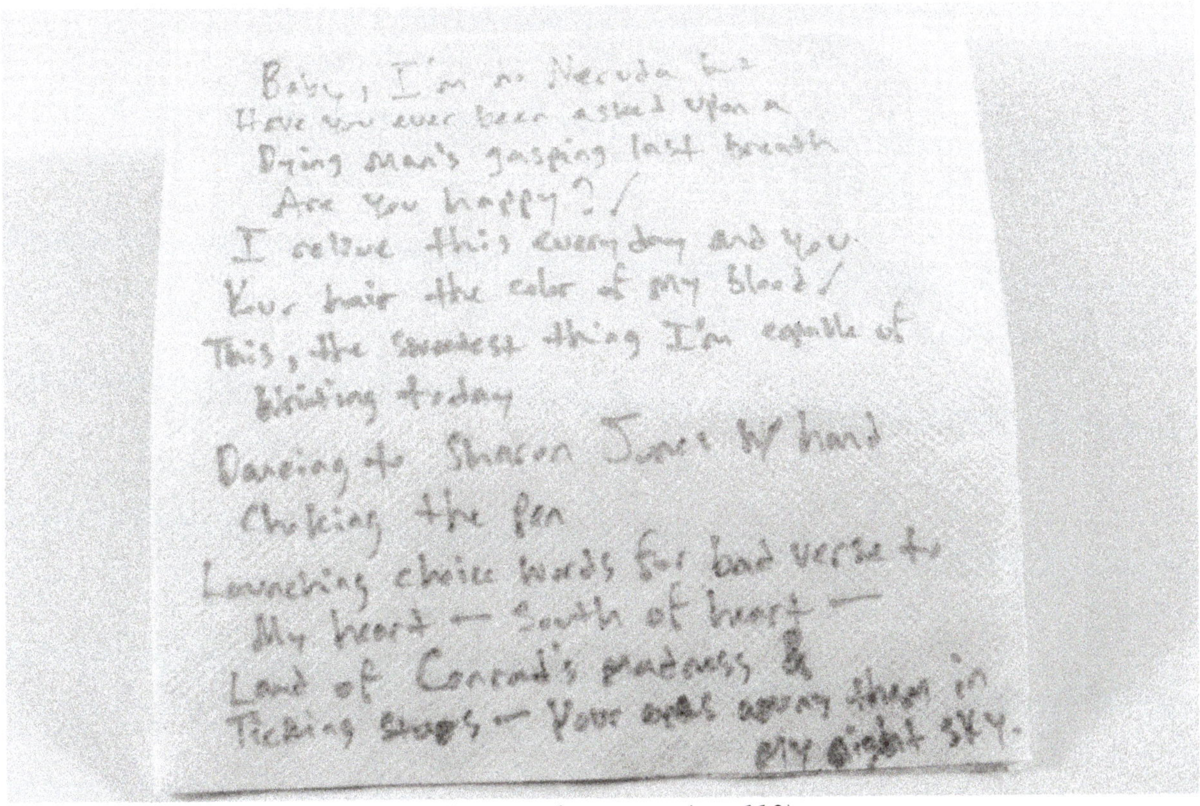

White-napkin poem (pg. 113)

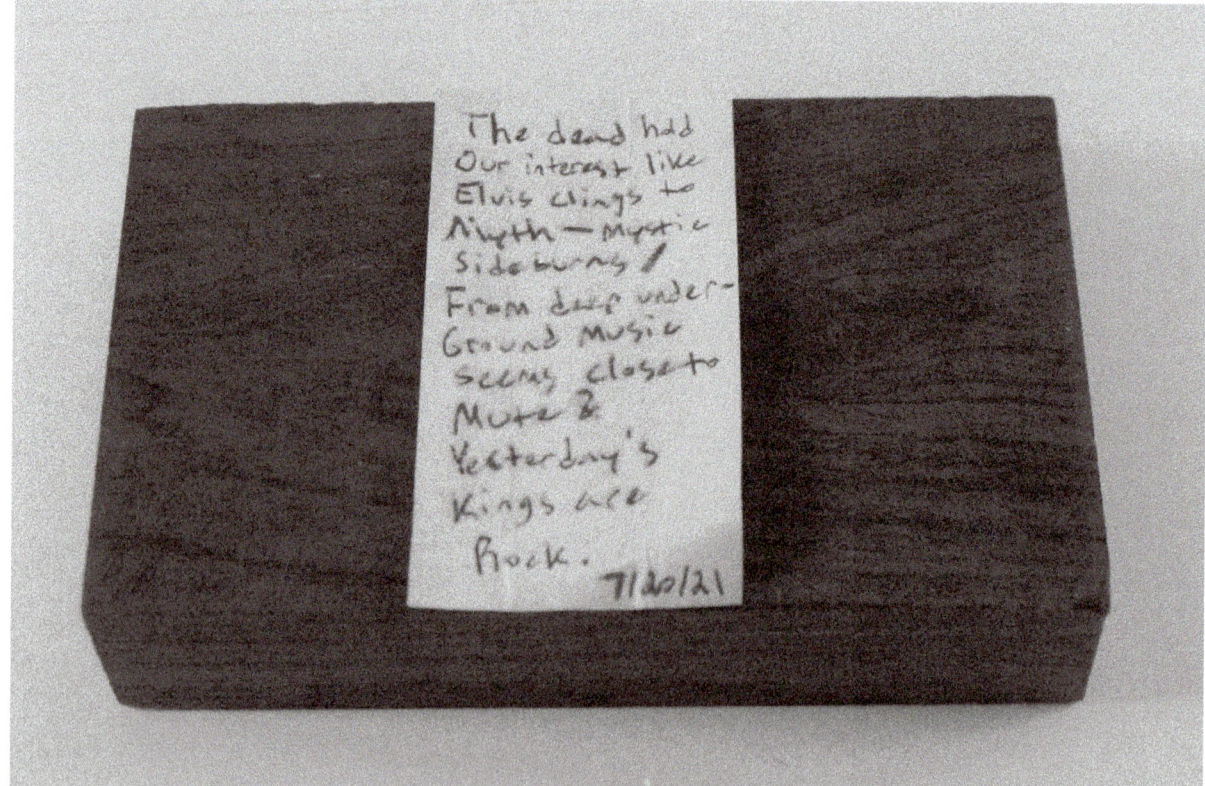

Brown-napkin poem No. 2 (pg. 113)

Gum-wrapper poem No. 12 (pg. 114)

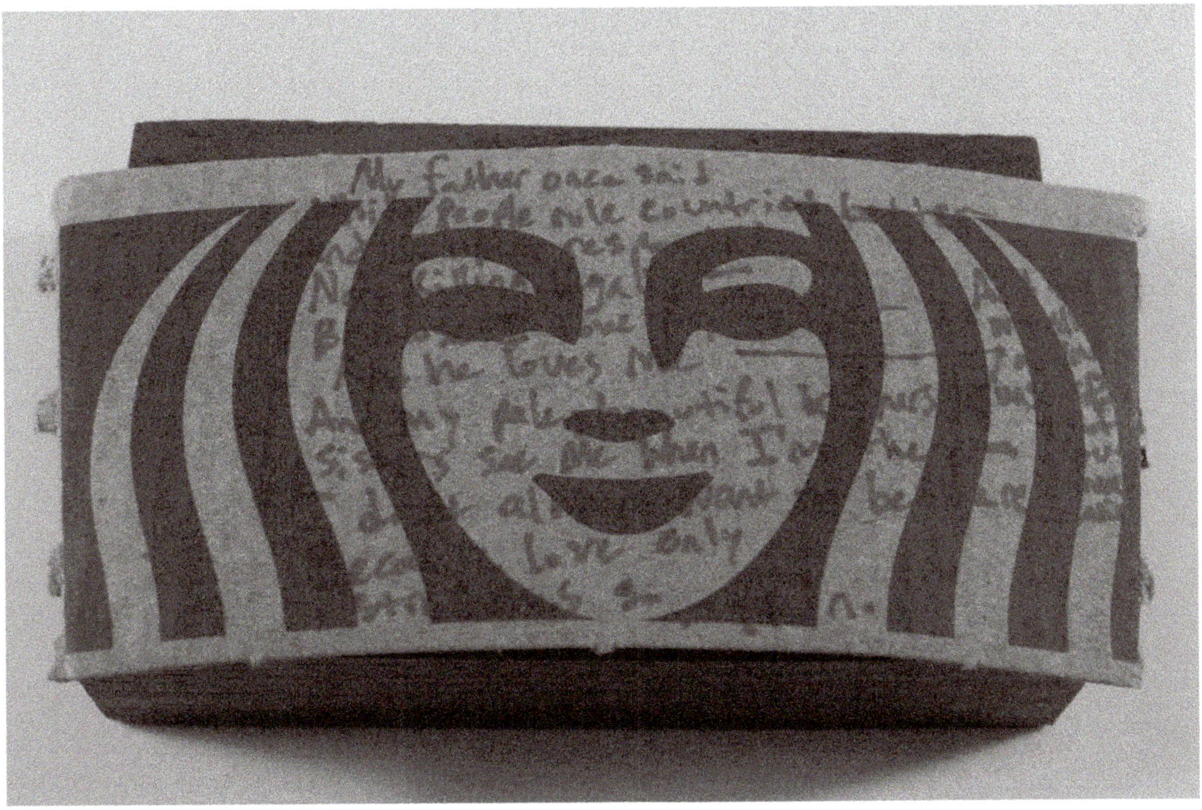
My father once said

Coffee-sleeve poem No. 6 (pg. 114)

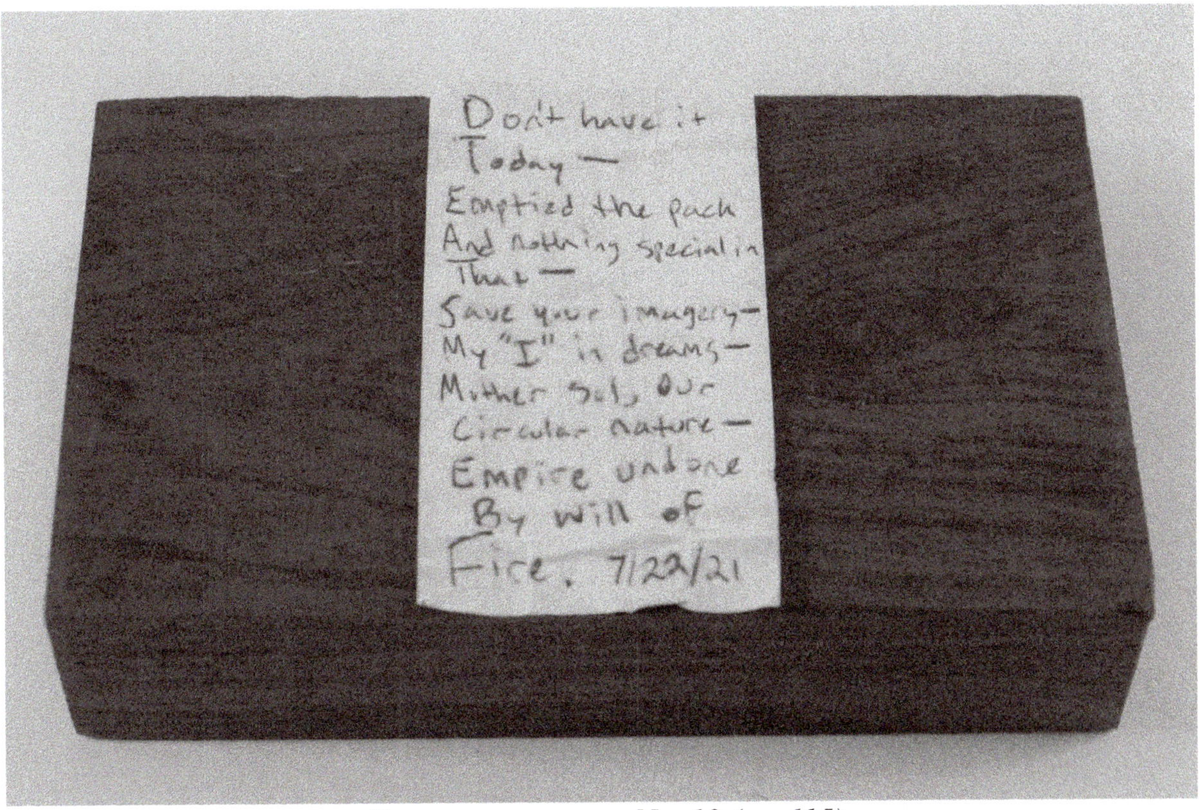
Don't have it
Today —
Emptied the pack
And nothing special in
That —
Save your imagery —
My "I" in dreams —
Mother Sol, Our
Circular nature —
Empire undone
By will of
Fire. 7/22/21

Gum-wrapper poem No. 13 (pg. 115)

Coffee-cup poem (pg. 115)

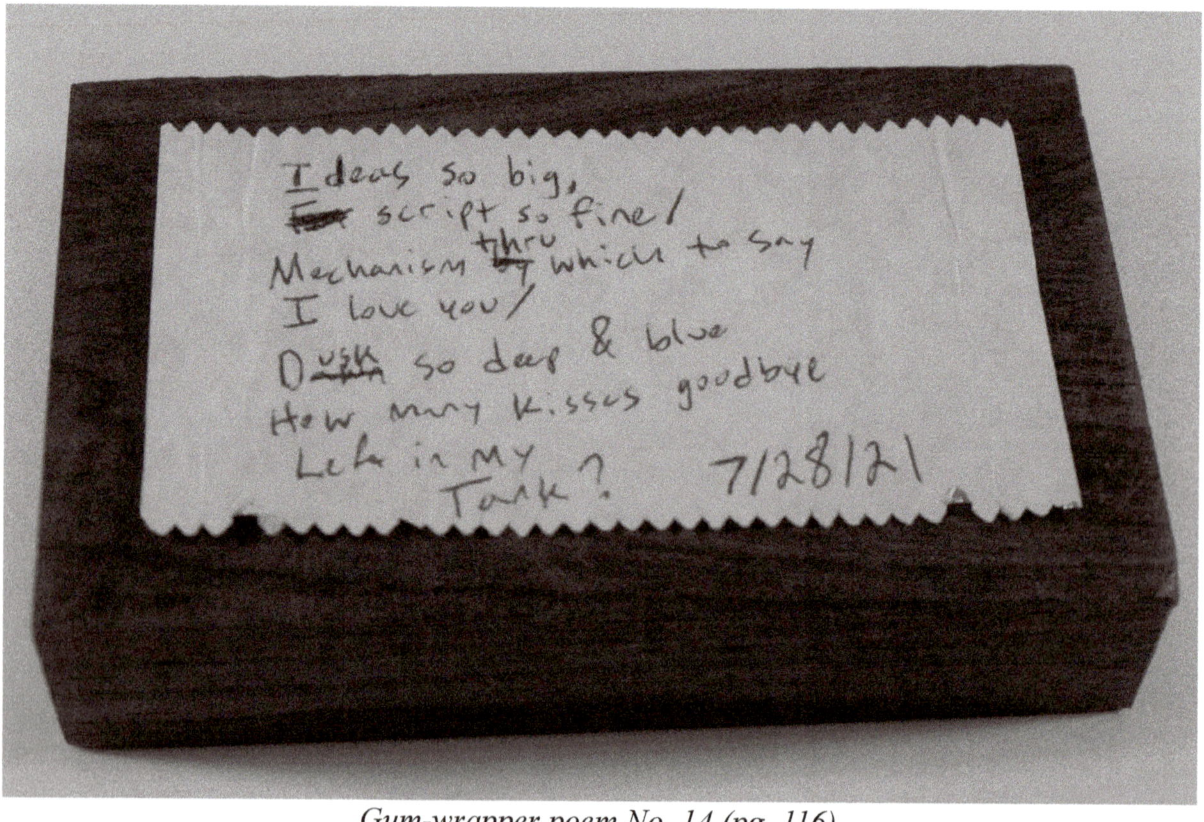

Gum-wrapper poem No. 14 (pg. 116)

Those who bemoan
Restless minds
Will be dust a
Long long time —
Live long in this
Silly compression
On this piece of trash
Held intact by laws
Beyond my grasp &
Adored by far 2 few —
To breath & move is

Reason for
Celebration.

7/30/21

Gum-wrapper poem No. 15 (pg. 116)

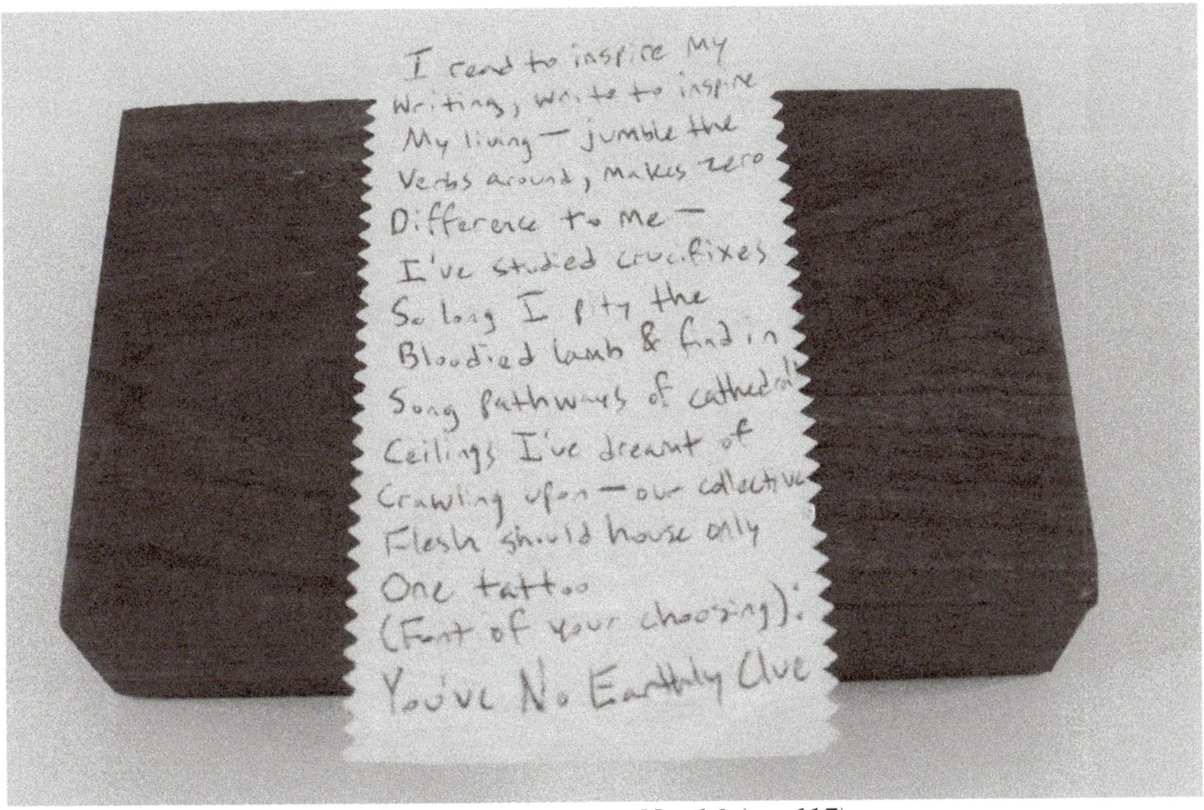

I read to inspire my
Writing, write to inspire
My living — jumble the
Verbs around, makes zero
Difference to me —
I've studied crucifixes
So long I pity the
Bloodied lamb & find in
Song pathways of cathedral
Ceilings I've dreamt of
Crawling upon — our collective
Flesh should house only
One tattoo
(Font of your choosing).
You've No Earthly Clue

Gum-wrapper poem No. 16 (pg. 117)

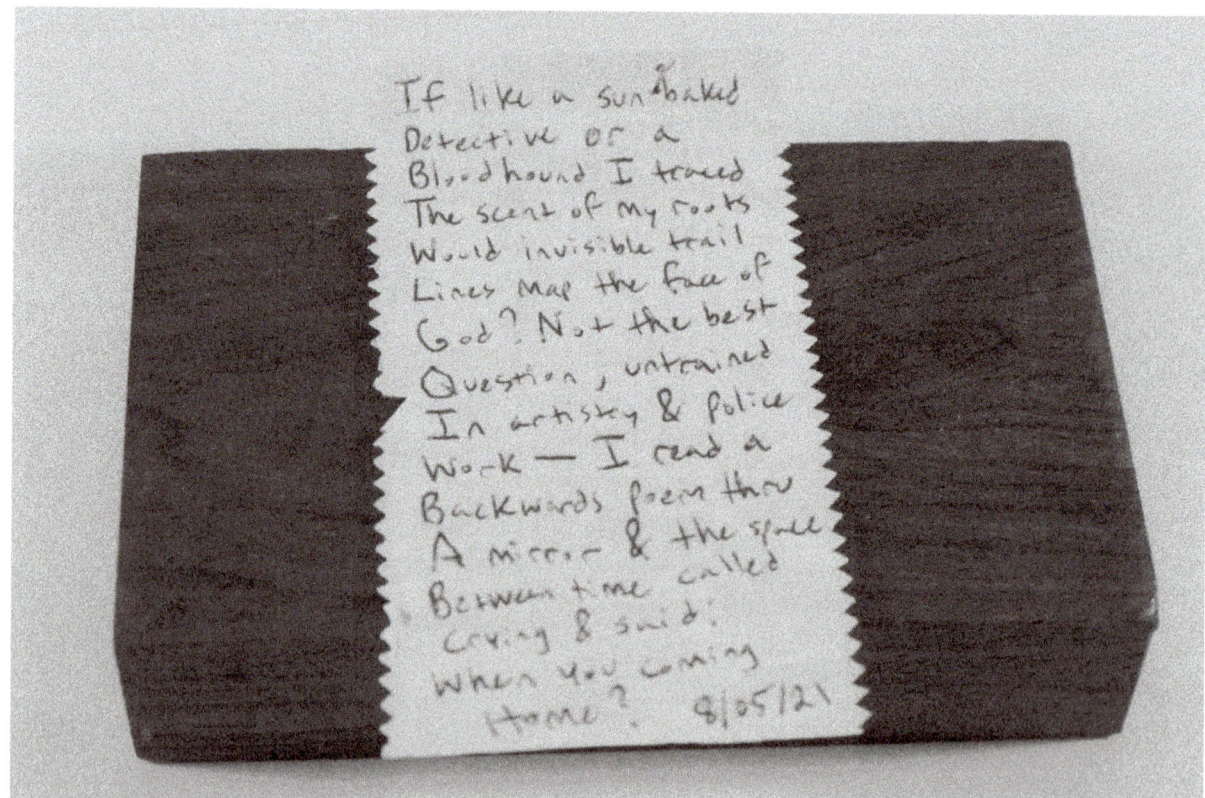

Brown-napkin poem No. 3 (pg. 117)

Gum-wrapper poem No. 17 (pg. 118)

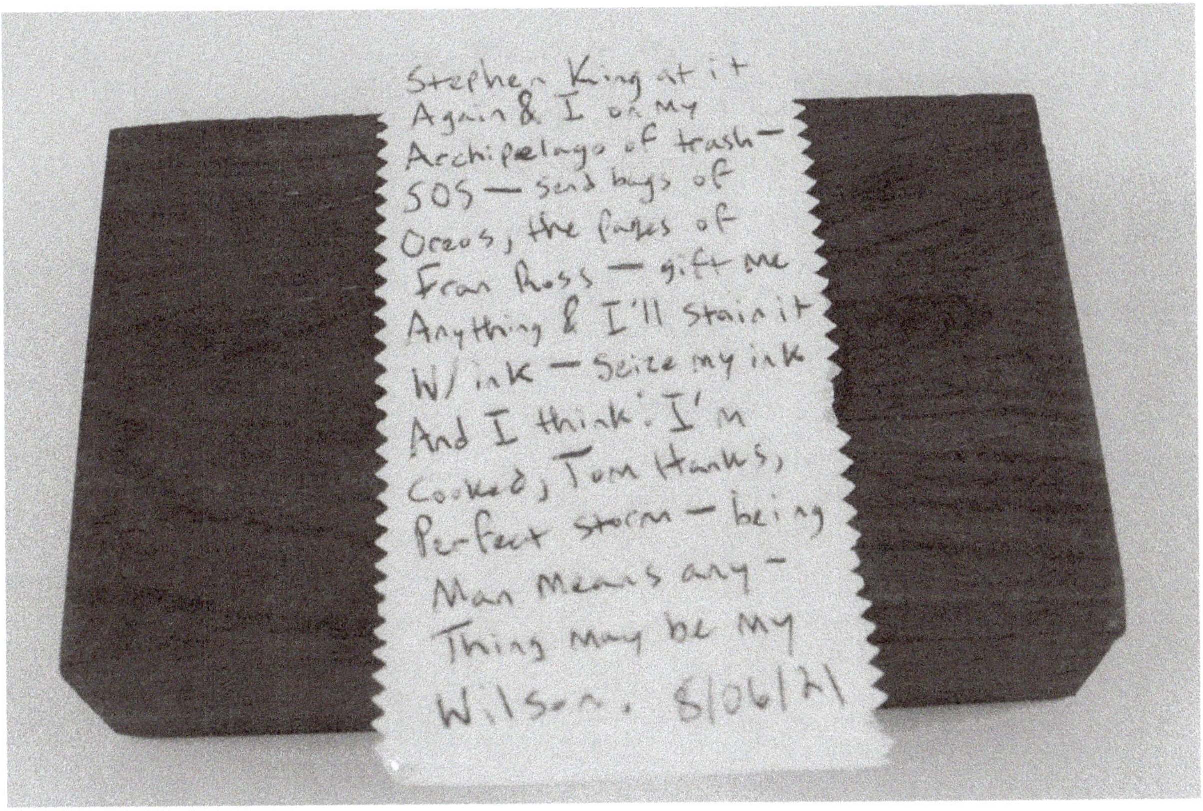

Stephen King at it
Again & I on my
Archipelago of trash—
SOS — send bags of
Oreos, the pages of
Fran Ross — gift me
Anything & I'll stain it
W/ ink — seize my ink
And I think: I'm
Cooked, Tom Hanks,
Perfect storm — being
Man means any—
Thing may be my
Wilson. 8/06/21

Gum-wrapper poem No. 18 (pg. 118)

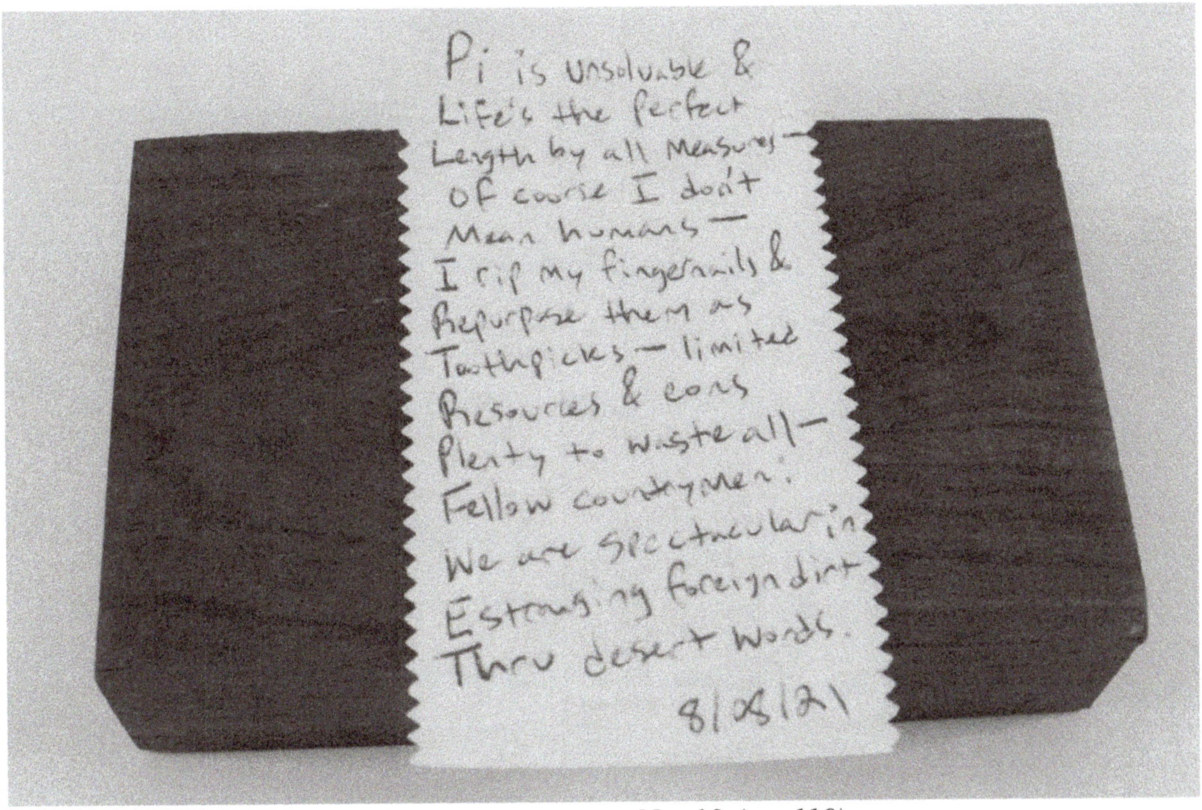

Pi is unsolvable &
Life's the perfect
Length by all measures—
Of course I don't
Mean humans —
I rip my fingernails &
Repurpose them as
Toothpicks. — limited
Resources & eons
Plenty to waste all—
Fellow countrymen:
We are spectacular in
Estrousing foreign dirt
Thru desert words.

8/08/21

Gum-wrapper poem No. 19 (pg. 119)

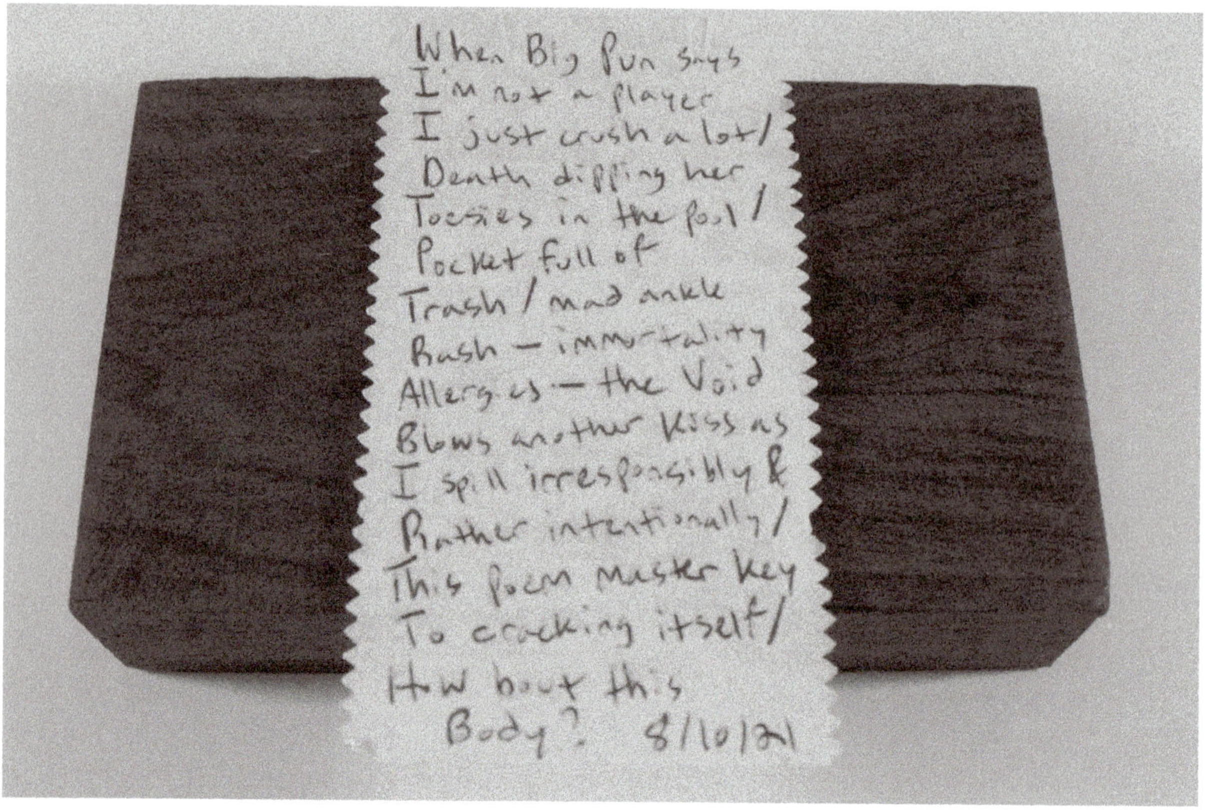

Gum-wrapper poem No. 20 (pg. 119)

When Big Pun says
I'm not a player
I just crush a lot/
Death dipping her
Toesies in the pool/
Pocket full of
Trash / mad ankle
Rash — immortality
Allergies — the Void
Blows another kiss as
I spill irresponsibly &
Rather intentionally/
This poem master key
To cracking itself/
How bout this
Body? 8/10/21

Gum-wrapper poem No. 21 (pg. 120)

When Hegel says
Too fair to worship
Too divine to love/
When Jesus says
Love your enemies
The sun rises on evil too/
When the sun says
Chase me &
Mourn the night/
When the moon says
I lift oceans to
Get a rise out of you.

8/11/21

McDonald's coffee-cup poem (pg. 120)

I told a friend recently I'm
Ashamed Ted Cruz owns a Spanish
Surname — and I'm ashamed for using
"Owns" and ashamed this is my 3rd
Poem featuring Cruz — but not ashamed
This is a trash poem, a spontaneous
Brown — napkin poem. A senator named
Cruz fled when ice settled in & folks
Froze to death in Texas. He could've
Been anyone but he is a
Cruz and I'm ashamed. How easily these
Words can be ash. How easily one can
Flee from a family poodle. Where is the
Honor, where is the love? Where's
Cruise control?

4/15/21

Brown-napkin poem No. 4 (pg. 121)

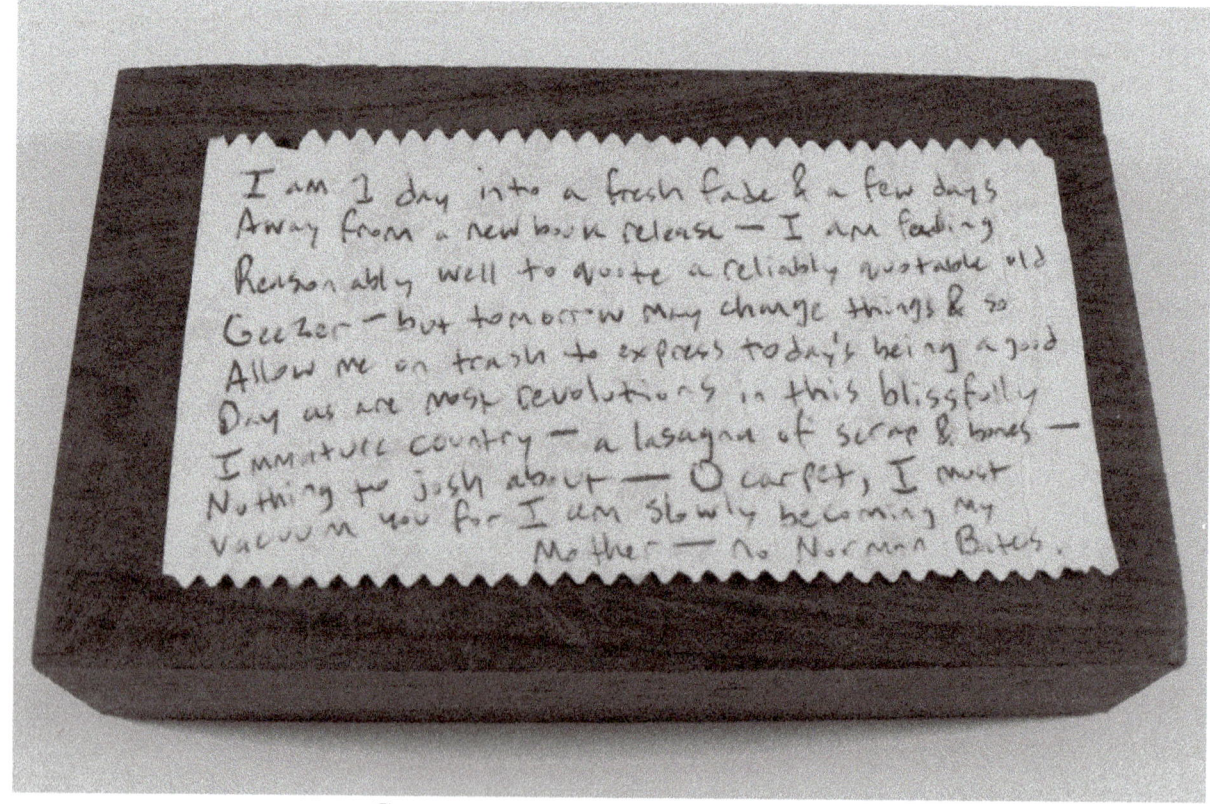

I am thankful I cannot see
At once
All (to quote Donald Barthelme)
The intersecting tendencies of
This world /
I am thankful for space /
Mine no different from yours /
I am thankful for governance — Its
Spasm of white-knuckled fear /
Pawns soldier up / Knuckles boned &
Bony like papa's — Salute /
I stretched so thin / heart skin of
A water balloon /
I am thankful for slow days at the
Office, the vacant kiss of a
Butterfly /
O Tunnel Vision, gorgeous green —
You give me room to bleed &
Write.

Brown-napkin poem No. 5 (pg. 121)

I am 1 day into a fresh fade & a few days
Away from a new book release — I am fading
Reasonably well to quote a reliably quotable old
Geezer — but tomorrow may change things & so
Allow me on trash to express today's being a good
Day as are most revolutions in this blissfully
Immature country — a lasagna of scrap & bones —
Nothing to josh about — O carpet, I must
Vacuum you for I am slowly becoming my
Mother — No Norman Bates.

Gum-wrapper poem No. 22 (pg. 122)

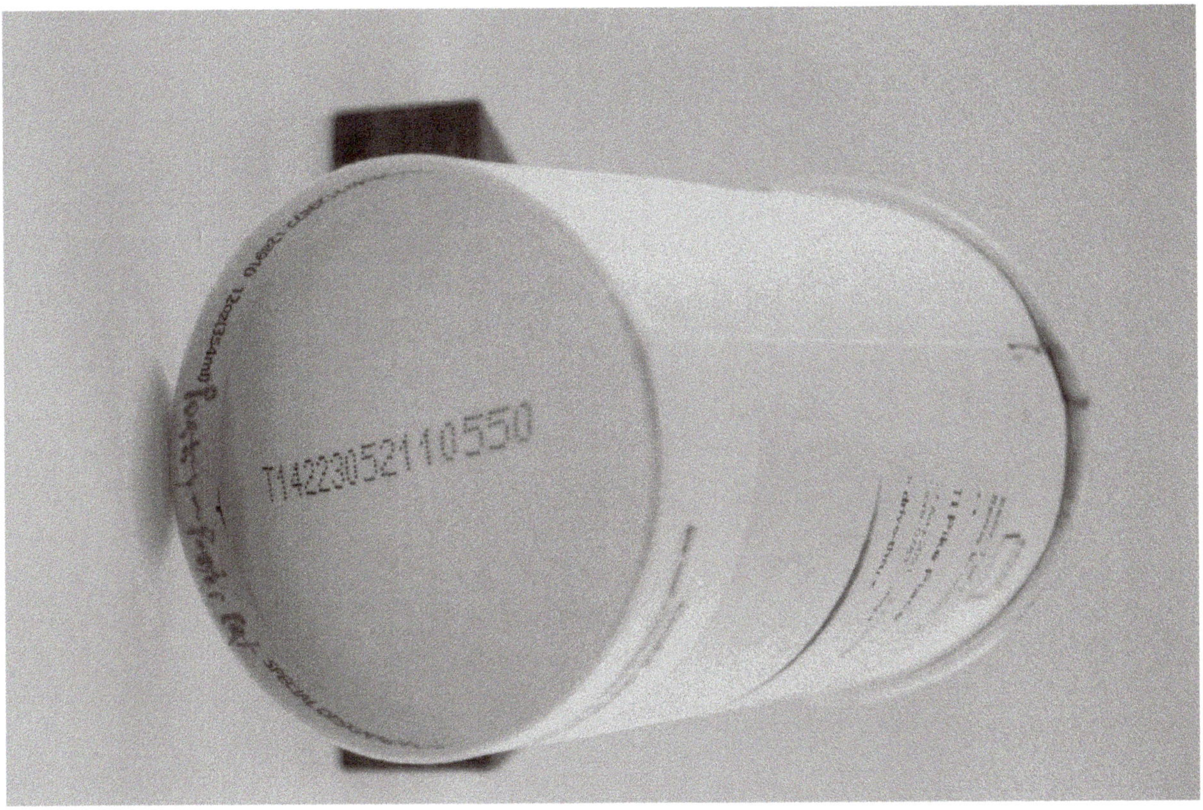
T14223052110550

Coffee-cup poem No. 3 (pg. 122)

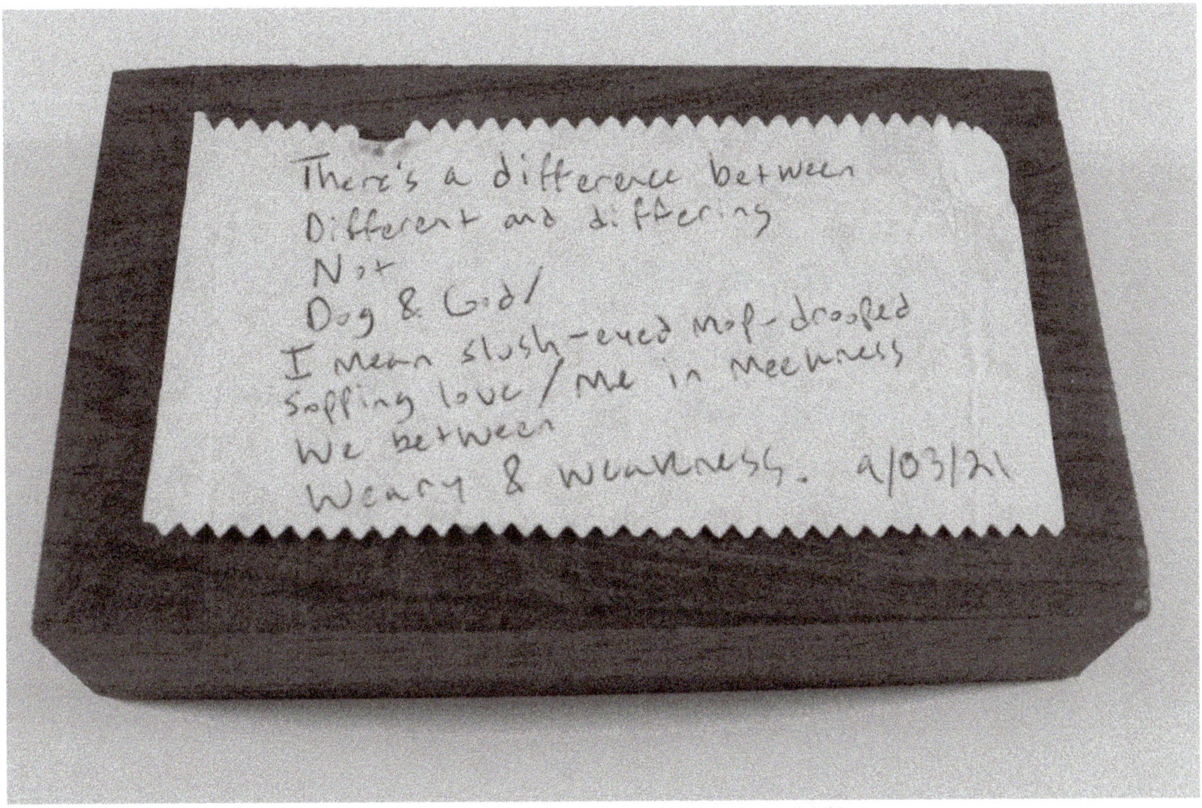
There's a difference between
Different and differing
Not
Dog & God/
I mean slush-eyed mop-drooped
sopping love / me in meekness
We between
Weary & weakness. 9/03/21

Gum-wrapper poem No. 23 (pg. 123)

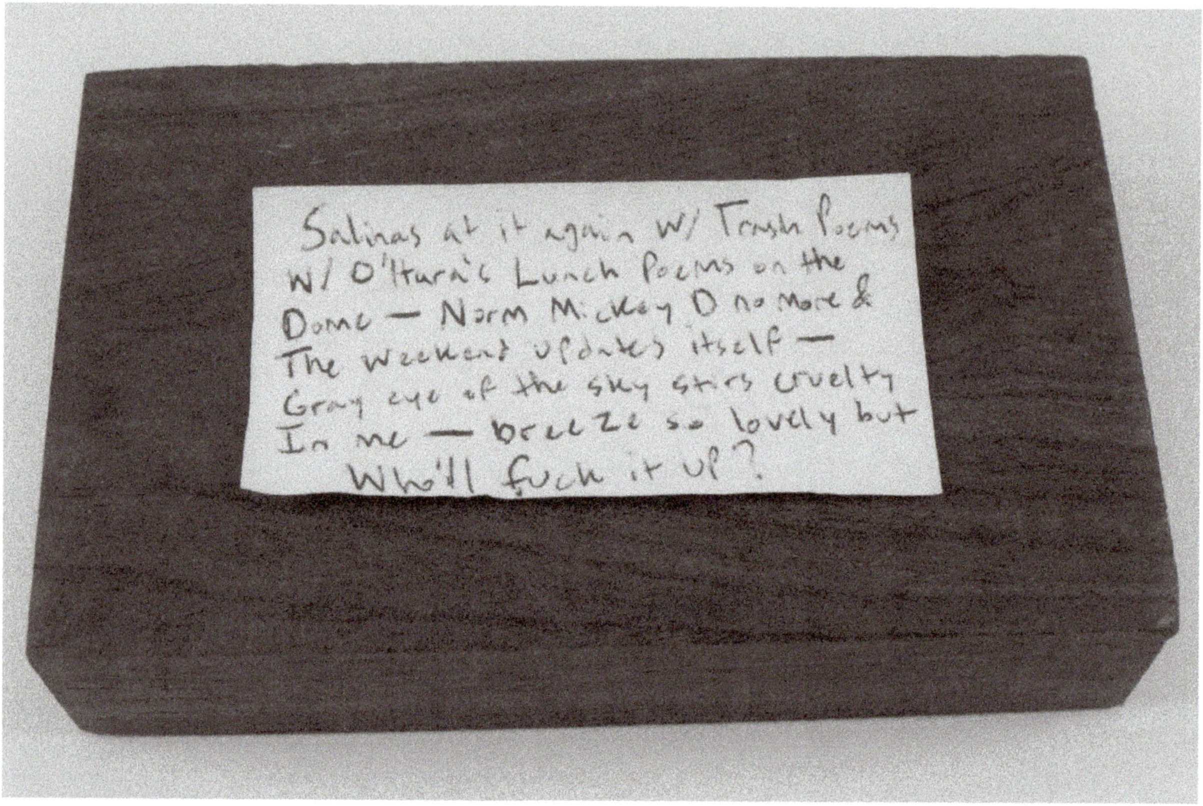

Gum-wrapper poem No. 24 (pg. 123)

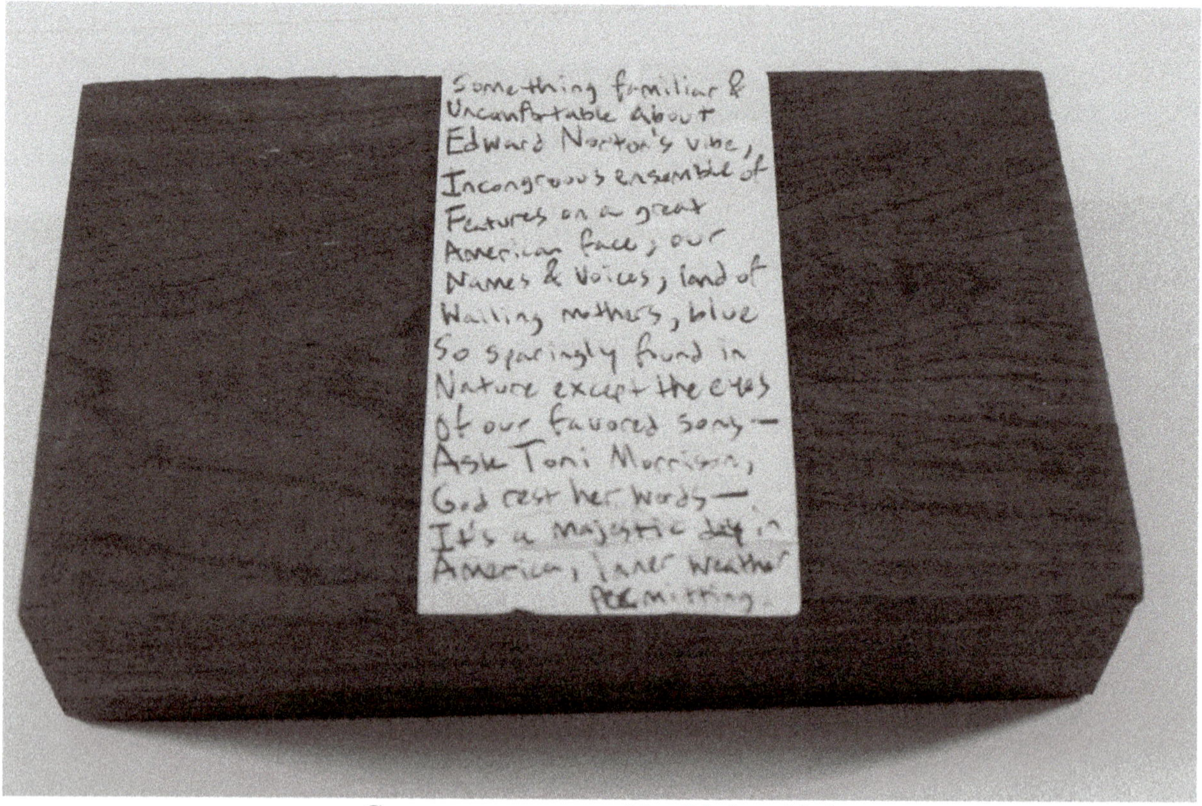

Gum-wrapper poem No. 25 (pg. 124)

Something about a loud voice in a cafe —
Follow me across the city
Across the collision of appetites —
Something about the space never felt right —
According to the pen all palms are tender
To the touch —
There aren't enough napkins for you —
The covering of mouths under gray clouds
Leaves eyes open to invasion —
Love as one prolonged sexy goodbye —
Here I trap the hopscotch of a man
In a parking lot
Who seems to embrace the familiar horror of
Rush hour as the cool air mummifies my throat
Making an instant snack outta my chewing gum
As I repeat these words aloud
Finding concealed stories in every crack
Between the teeth of the earth,
And did I mention

There aren't enough napkins?
The madman across a 4-way
Conducting it w/ jazz fingers &
The baton of invisible notes.

Brown-napkin poem No. 6 (pg. 124)

Brown-napkin poem No. 7 (pg. 125)

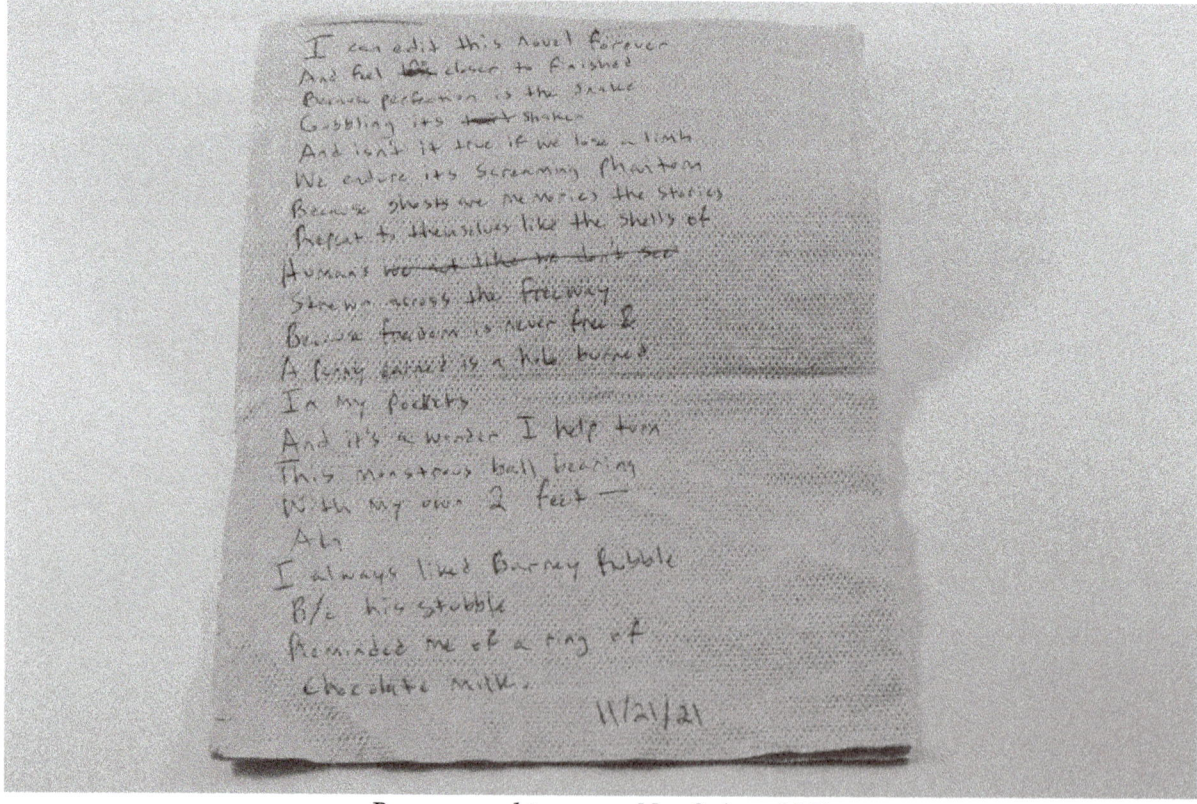

Brown-napkin poem No. 8 (pg. 125)

Arms wide open into
A new day in America
Caffeinated. Amped up.
Schools scratching the itch
Stop & go. Red, green & yellow.
Bolivia. Lithuania. Congo.
We're really doing it. We've done it now
Leaving ourselves behind.
A scrap. A line. Flesh recurring in dreams.
Genius n.bodies 2-stepping around us.
The pull of city lights. The country's
Belly where our blood is buried.
Wanda Coleman haunted by Neruda
Whispering his name. Astral projections
For the birds. Splatter your insides out
The page. Take my job. I'm halfway teasing.
Poems straddling you to the finish line
Shaped like threats. Do not feed the
Man with the pen — he, among the
Animals
Where the price is too high.

Brown-napkin poem No. 9 (pg. 126)

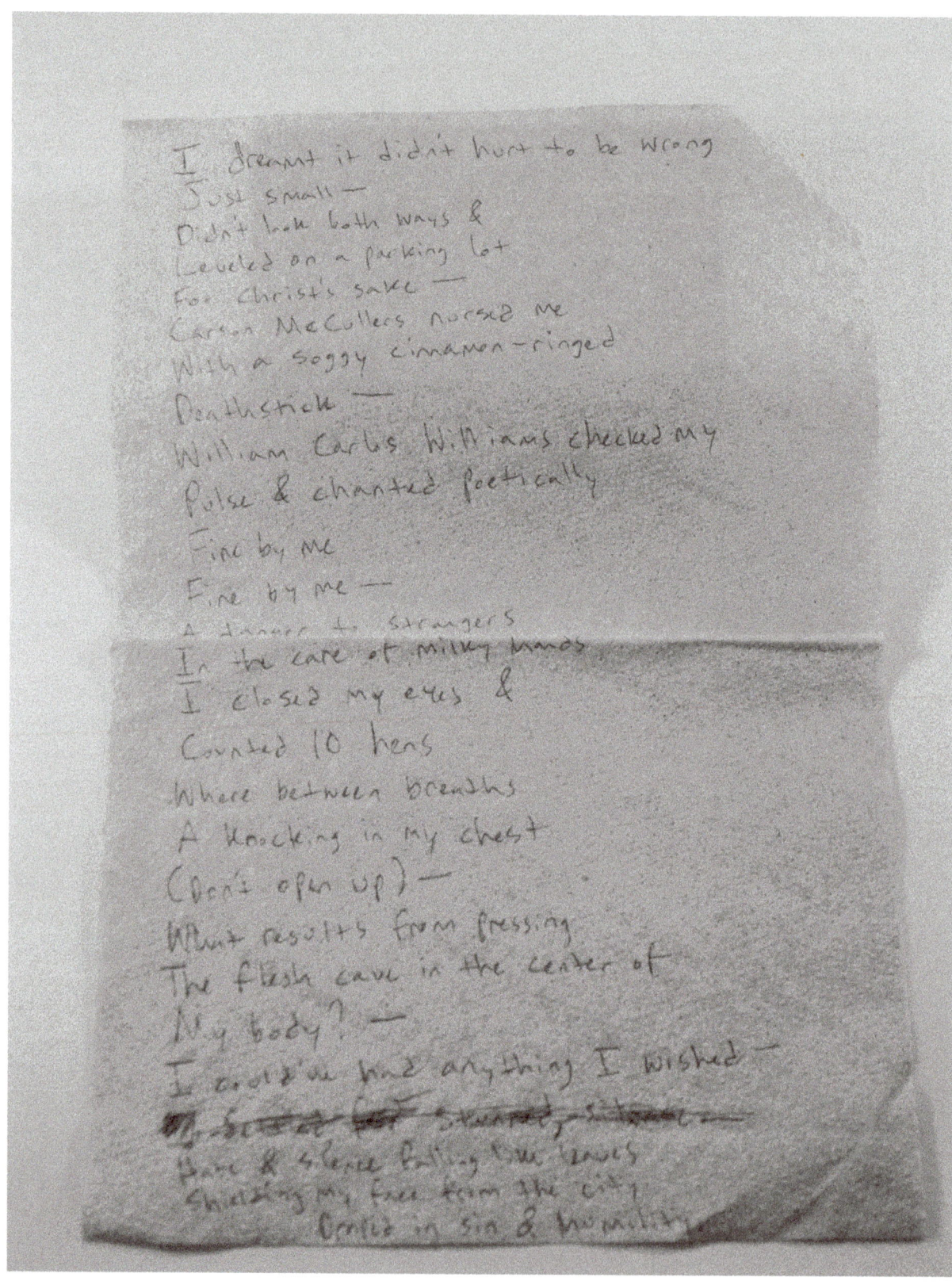

Brown-napkin poem No. 10 (pg. 127)

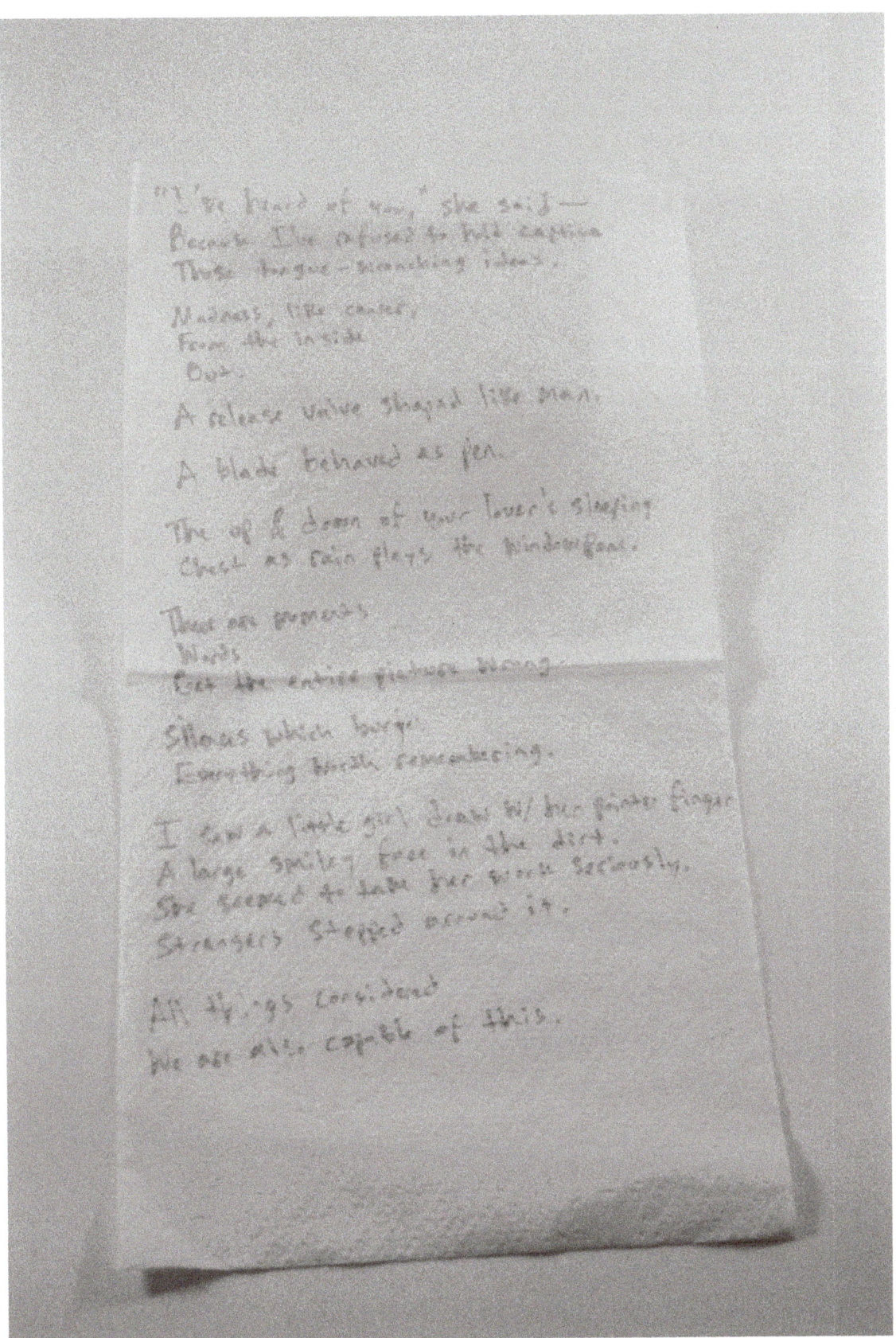

White-napkin poem No. 2 (pg. 128)

White-napkin poem No. 3 (pg. 129)

White-napkin poem No. 4 (pg. 130)

Gum-wrapper poem No. 26 (pg. 130)

Learn the language

Its peculiar rhythms

Nothing's fixed

Not words tattooed on skin

Nas said you're heaven-sent

Not a metaphor for me

Funny papers framed w/ cheap desire

Pesos on the flimsy dollar

Sea-foam wings in vanilla sky

Nonburn candles w/o time

Nice one, chief

This music won't bewitch itself

The overtoraved "I" in divine

I can change a tire but can I define the

Difference between unbelievable & un–

Deniable w/o ~~——~~ breaking a few eggs for

The ~~~~ Omelette of the 4th Wall?

The period as a blink & a breath

The period as double dare to

Swallow that bullet on your tongue.

Brown-napkin poem No. 11 (pg. 131)

Gum-wrapper poem No. 27 (pg. 132)

Coffee-sleeve poem No. 7 (pg. 132)

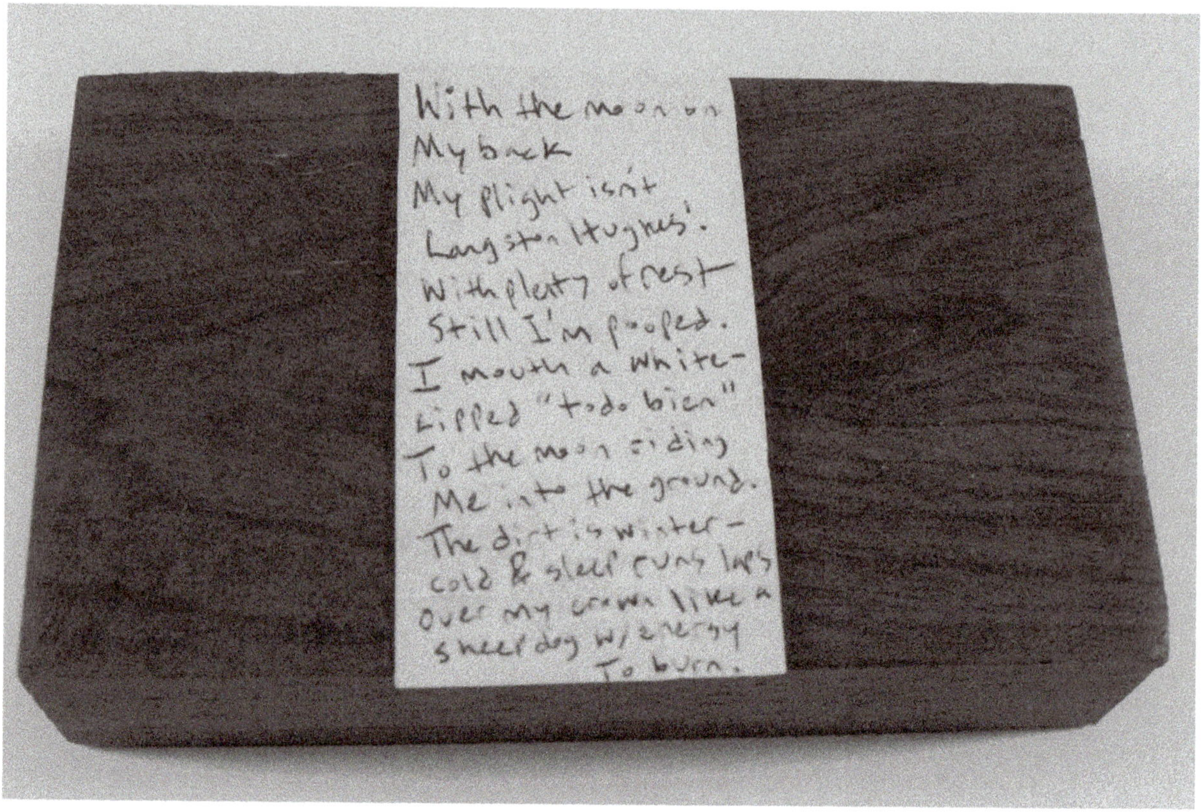

Gum-wrapper poem No. 28 (pg. 133)

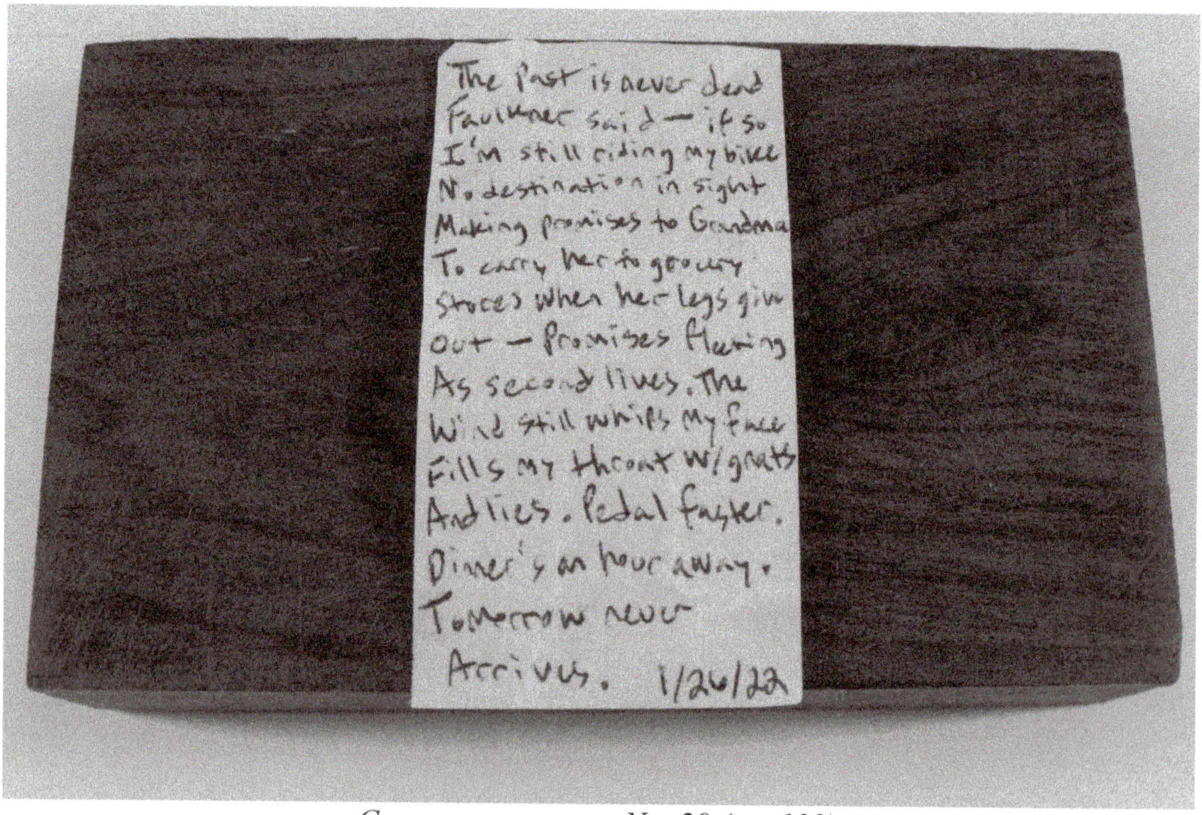

With the moon on
My back
My plight isn't
Langston Hughes'.
With plenty of rest
Still I'm pooped.
I mouth a white-
Lipped "todo bien"
To the moon riding
Me into the ground.
The dirt is winter-
cold & sleet runs lines
over my crown like a
sheep dog w/ energy
To burn.

Gum-wrapper poem No. 29 (pg. 133)

The past is never dead
Faulkner said — if so
I'm still riding my bike
No destination in sight
Making promises to Grandma
To carry her to grocery
stores when her legs give
Out — promises flaring
As second lives. The
Wind still whirls my face
Fills my throat w/ gnats
And lies. Pedal faster.
Dinner's an hour away.
Tomorrow never
Arrives.   1/26/22

Today is one of those days
In which every 5 minutes
I can drop my backpack & run.
From what? Surely not my fixed
Perspective — not the toxin inside
From which I mine these words
Nourishing & suffocating steadily.
A poet friend once penned himself
Out of death only to be locked in a
Page. All I have left of him:
His signature & a PDF document of
His last (unpublished) book
Which I cannot bring myself to finish.
I can hardly bring myself to escape
Though not once have I regretted
The decisions I've made
Which I made the best that I could.
The small joy of a water fountain
Drowning out pretentious shoppers' chatter.
The simple pleasure of being asked to
Sign my book at a local bookstore.
What goes unread is the same as
What goes unsaid. (It goes w/o saying.)
The point of breath & noise is to enjoy
The total embrace of coming silence.
I will save dying for tomorrow.
For here & now, my ears are open.

Brown-napkin poem No. 12 (pg. 134)

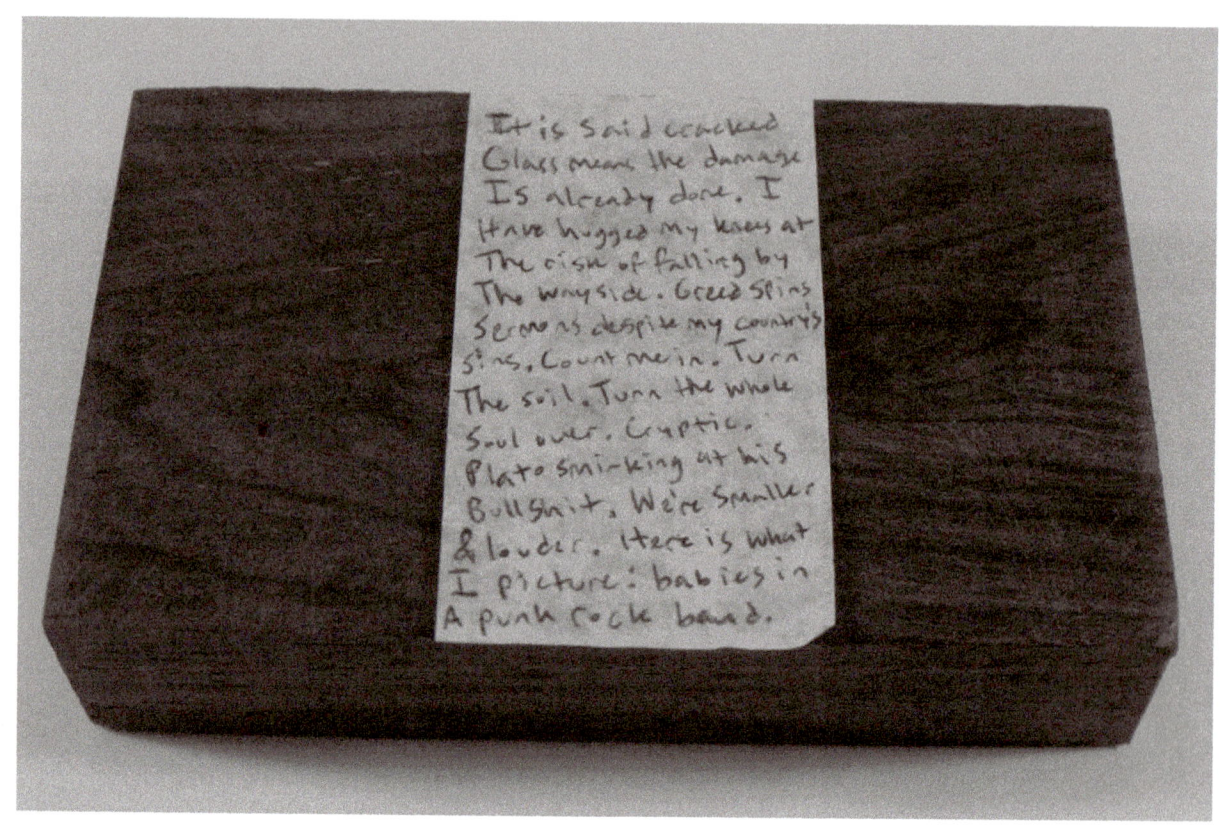

Gum-wrapper poem No. 30 (pg. 135)

When Alex Ebert sings
She got super cute lips
I understand the image because the women of
My page are perfect when — only when —
The darkness shuts my eyes.

Because sharp teeth. Electricity.

Shortages in the city.

A city's only noisy
If our own
Guesses our stars.

Medium suggestive in 3 tongues.

Income — there are two ya.
How can one sit so still
But still
Be on the run.

(Do not buy a gun.)

Frightened & busy in the city.
Someone in a suit thinks he's threading needles fueled by
Potent rainbow pills.
In the city
My muscles won't work.

I read about our city from my library where each book
Is more dangerous than the last. How we got here is
A long & complicated story. I'm willing to believe
Angels will fall from the sky & suck our oceans so long as
My suspension of disbelief is sufficient by guns & stars—
Soaked cages obscuring my view of the plains where it is said
People of faith dance around a campfire.

The song of love & death in the city,
Can you hear me sing from the shower?
Only in this poem do I sound like Fitches Unless.
The throat has a cracked runway. / The note as a
Puzzling Beethoven

I invest in this neighbor to the extent that they
Turbocharge the views simulation.

Ooh.

If you've named / personified your vehicle —
Your lemon, your carriage, your crick magnet, your buggy, your bike —
Welcome to the city built just for us.

Stay on your side. Join my team. Come inside to apply.
No experience necessary. Stick around & the lies
Moisturize your skin to where everything slides off you
Like an interception the conjecture in heavenly salvation.

There's only so many lives that can survive on this napkin.
Never mind that it's white.

All the better to witness our messes.

2/04/22

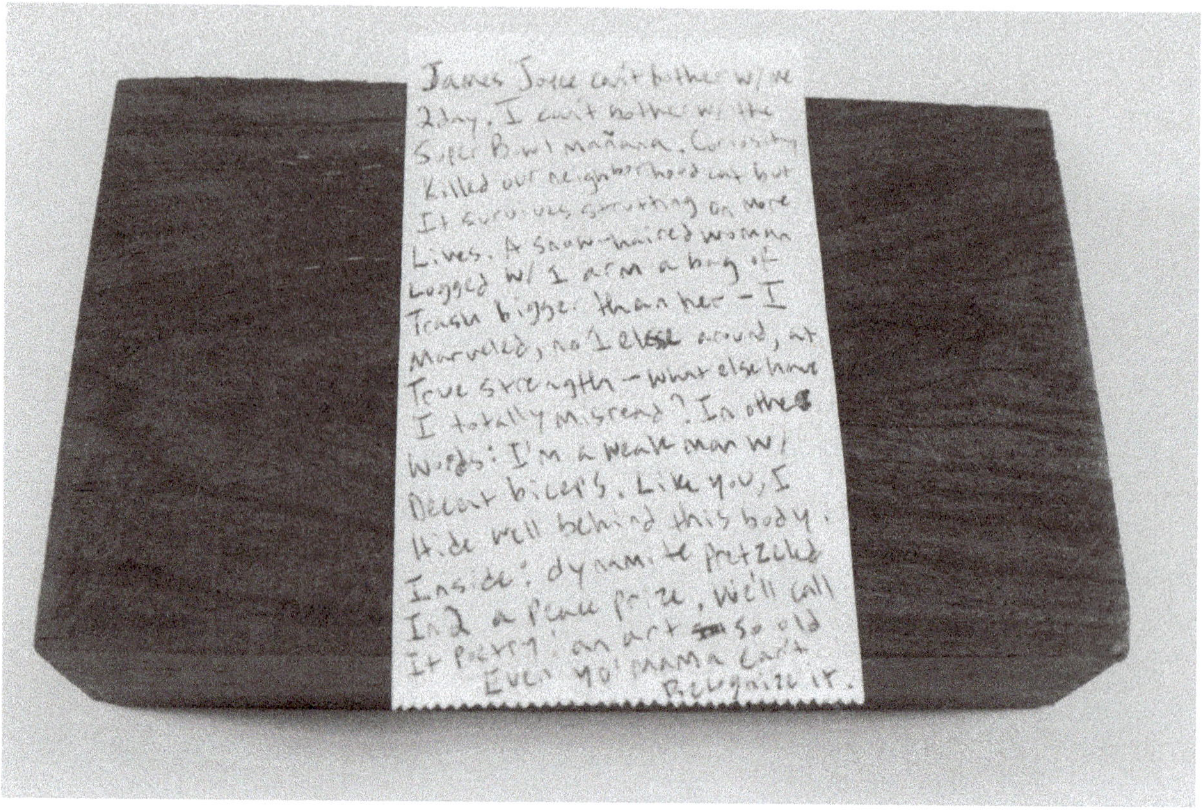

Receipt poem No. 1 (pg. 137)

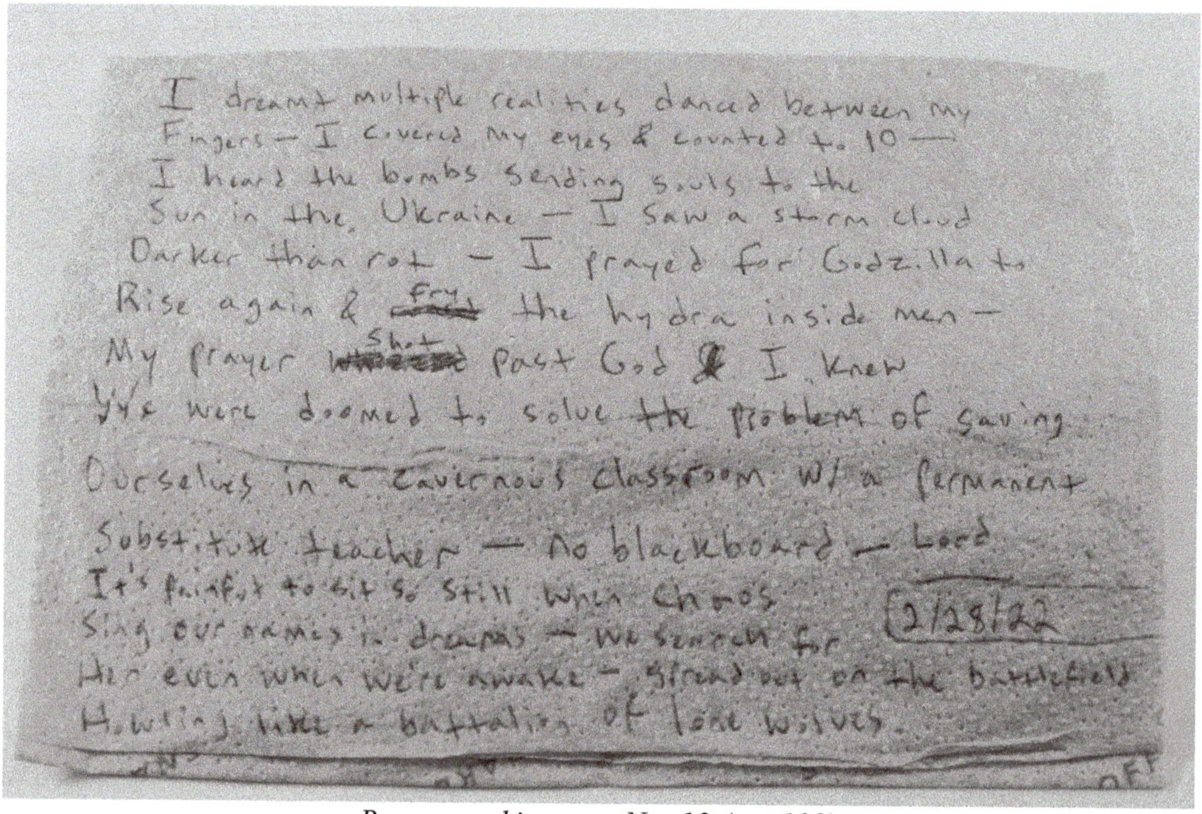

James Joyce can't bother w/ me 2day, I can't bother w/ the Super Bowl mañana. Curiosity killed our neighborhood cat but it survives sprouting on more lives. A snow-haired woman lugged w/ 1 arm a bag of trash bigger than her — I marveled, no 1 else around, at true strength — what else have I totally misread? In other words: I'm a weak man w/ decent biceps. Like you, I hide well behind this body. Inside: dynamite pretzels. In 2 a peace prize, we'll call it pretty, an art so old even yo' mama can't recognize it.

Brown-napkin poem No. 13 (pg. 138)

I dreamt multiple realities danced between my fingers — I covered my eyes & counted to 10 — I heard the bombs sending souls to the sun in the Ukraine — I saw a storm cloud darker than rot — I prayed for Godzilla to rise again & fry the hydra inside men — My prayer shot past God & I knew we were doomed to solve the problem of saving ourselves in a cavernous classroom w/ a permanent substitute teacher — No blackboard — Lord it's painful to sit so still when chaos sing our armies to dreams — we search for her even when we're awake — spread out on the battlefield howling like a battalion of lone wolves. 2/28/22

I thought by today
I'd have something more significant
To say —
~~So~~ Unbearable illiteracy rates
Creeps in suits & black robes
Legalese picking clean the bones
Love tainted & plucked from the
Collective tongue
~~And~~ The rising cost of grief therapy —
Nope — I bought a John Updike
Novel for 50 cents at a bookstore whose
Primary source of income comes from Magic
Cards — I gave the owner a dollar & said
"Keep the change" — Like I was
Doing her a
Favor.

White-napkin poem No. 6 (pg. 138)

"Get up from the floor, guys," a father chirps at his young sons,
And I wonder if, years later, the boy, now a man,
Reads a tattered book from the ground, lying on his back,
An old book he found at an antiques shop, pure chance,
A nearly forgotten book his wife insists discovered him,
For when it comes to literature the relationship is one-
Directional, a river transporting the deeds ~~and~~ hopes &
Dreams setting ~~us~~ apart in the kingdom of God, so it is said,
And how effortlessly a book in the river's care becomes a
Smattering of crinkled ink, and even that ~~too~~ changes, leaving us
With the fact of the river, the fragility of paper words, though
They live on mangled in our minds, fables battered by a game
Of Telephone, and I want to be able to recognize the book
~~The boy'll someday read,~~ the book which swims its way to
Him — but I'm ~~a~~ afraid this is one detail I cannot
Manage on this beautiful day, & so I'll carry it with me
In accordance with the laws of nature, which I am
Barely beginning to understand,
Let alone accept.

03/25/22

Brown-napkin poem No. 14 (pg. 139)

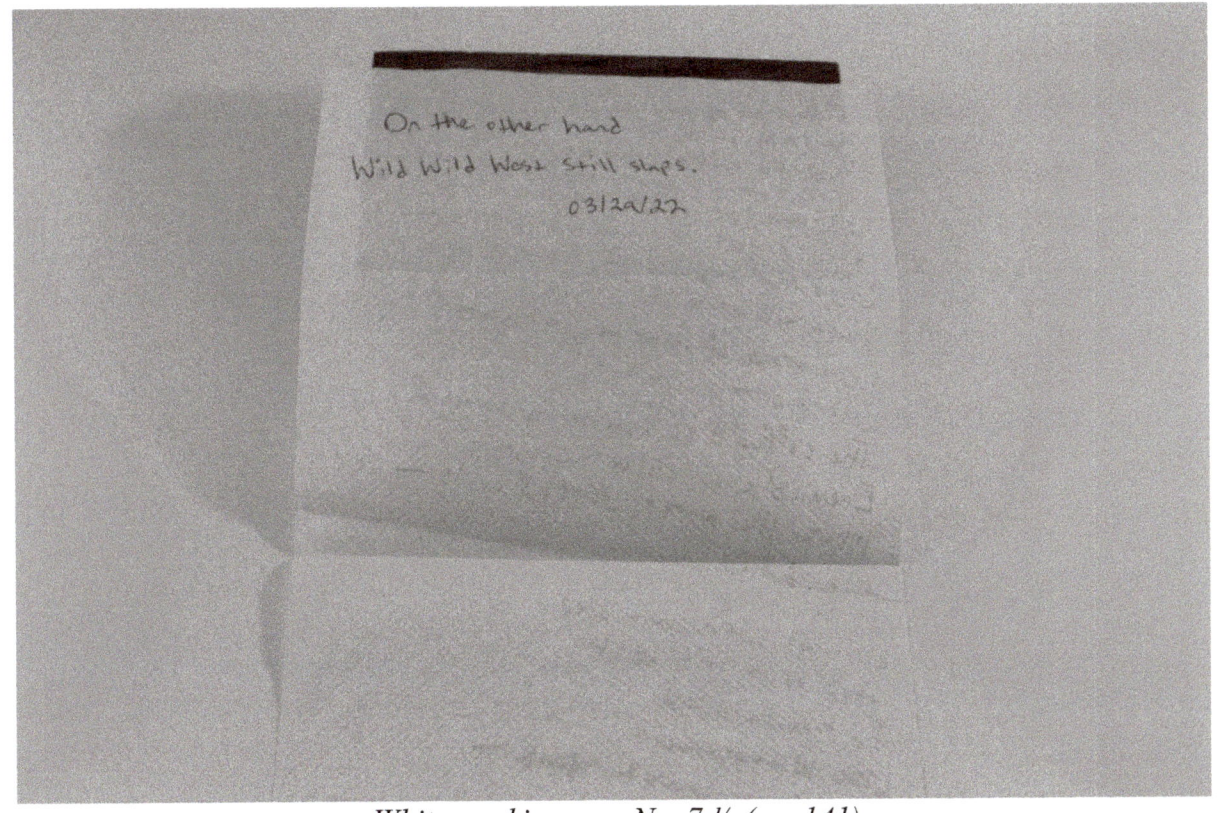

White-napkin poem No. 7 (pg. 140)

White-napkin poem No. 7 ½ (pg. 141)

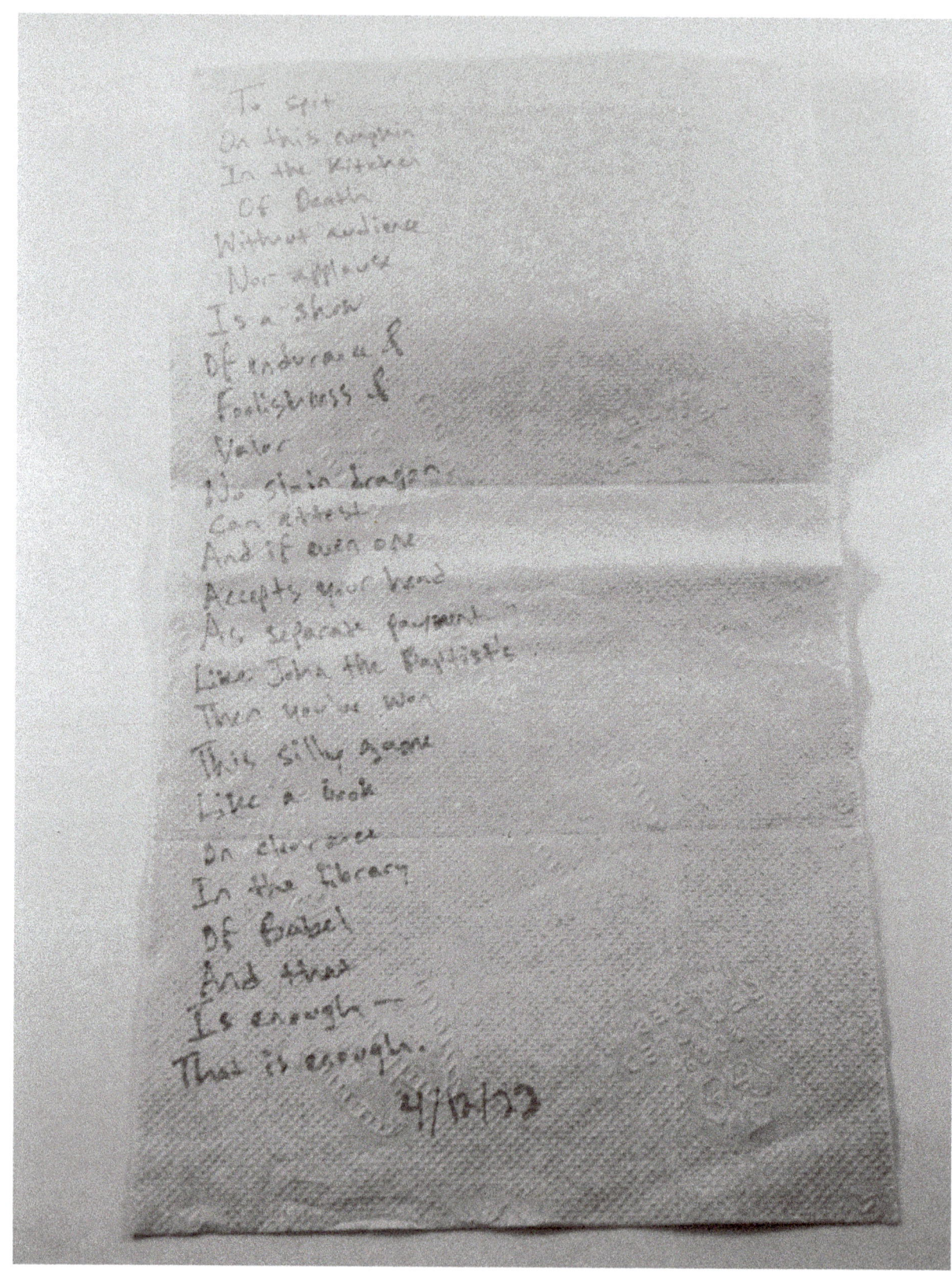

Brown-napkin poem No. 15 (pg. 141)

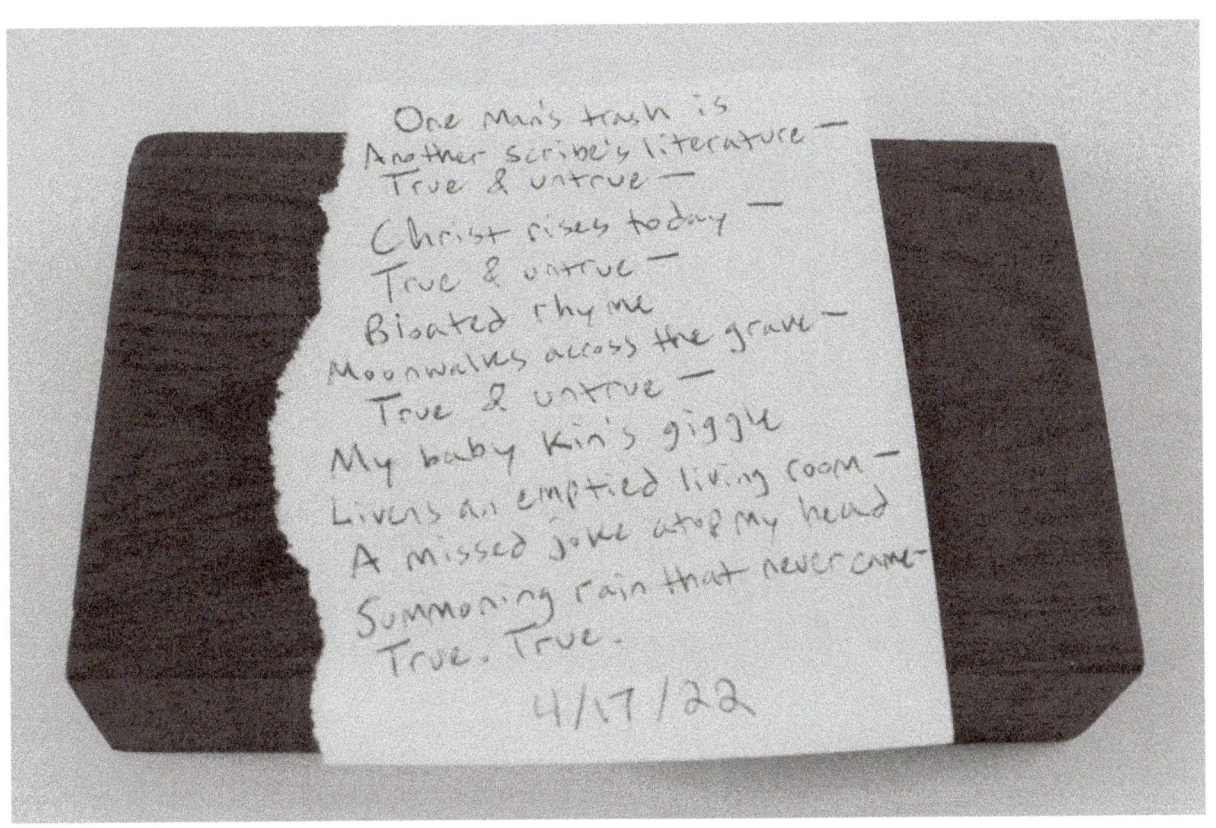

Receipt poem No. 2 (pg. 142)

Campbell's Soup-can poem (pg. 142)

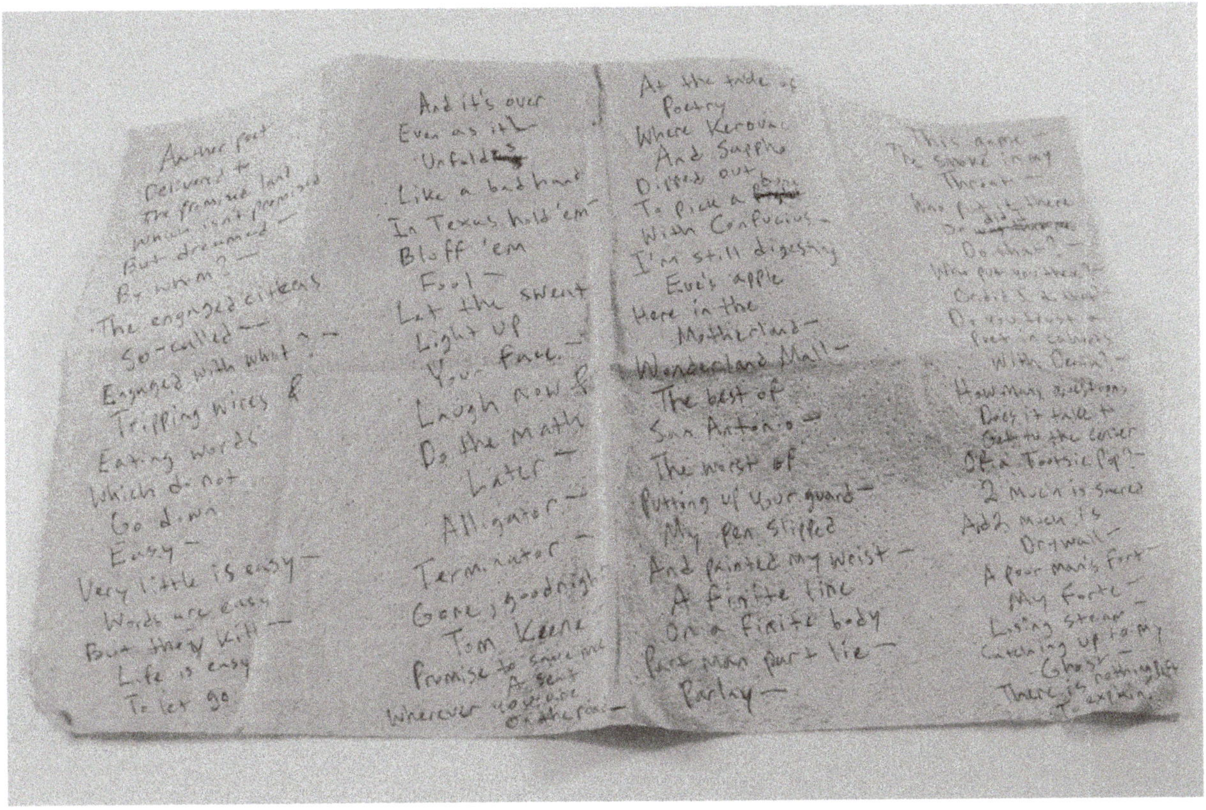

Brown-napkin poem No. 16 (pg. 143)

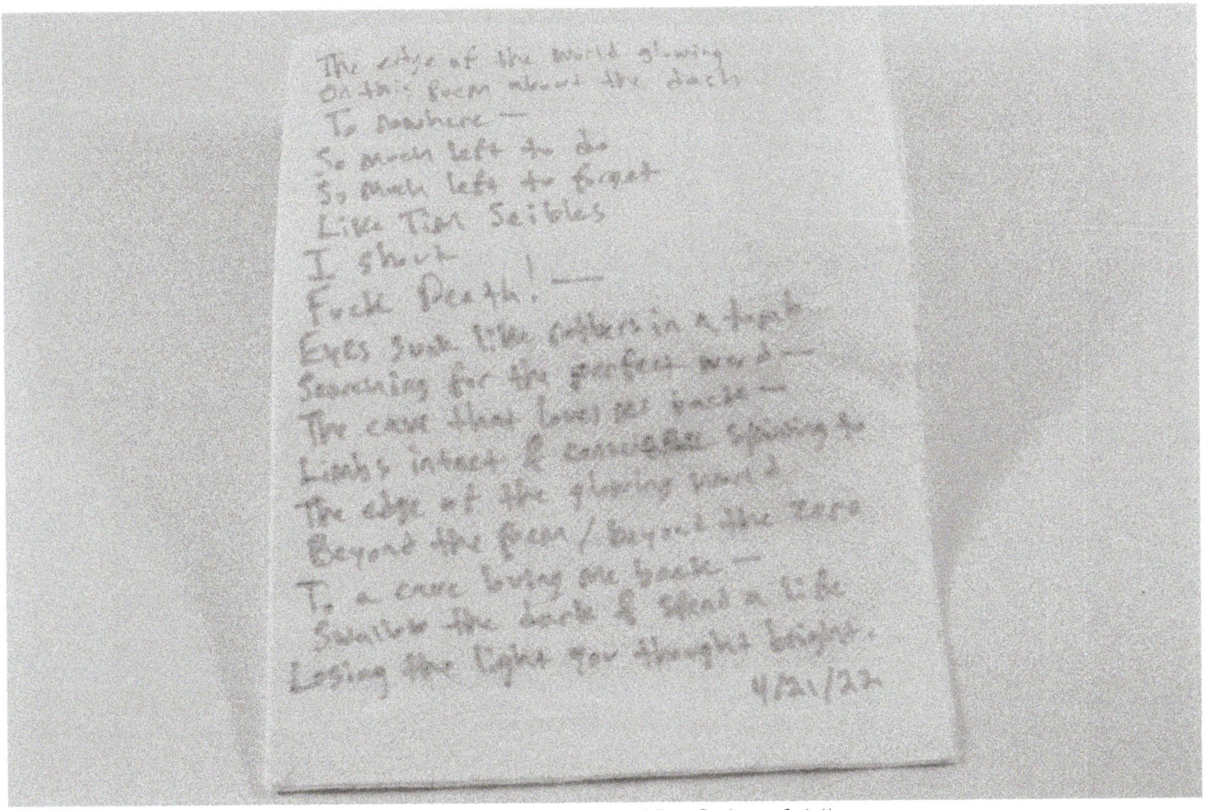

White-napkin poem No. 8 (pg. 144)

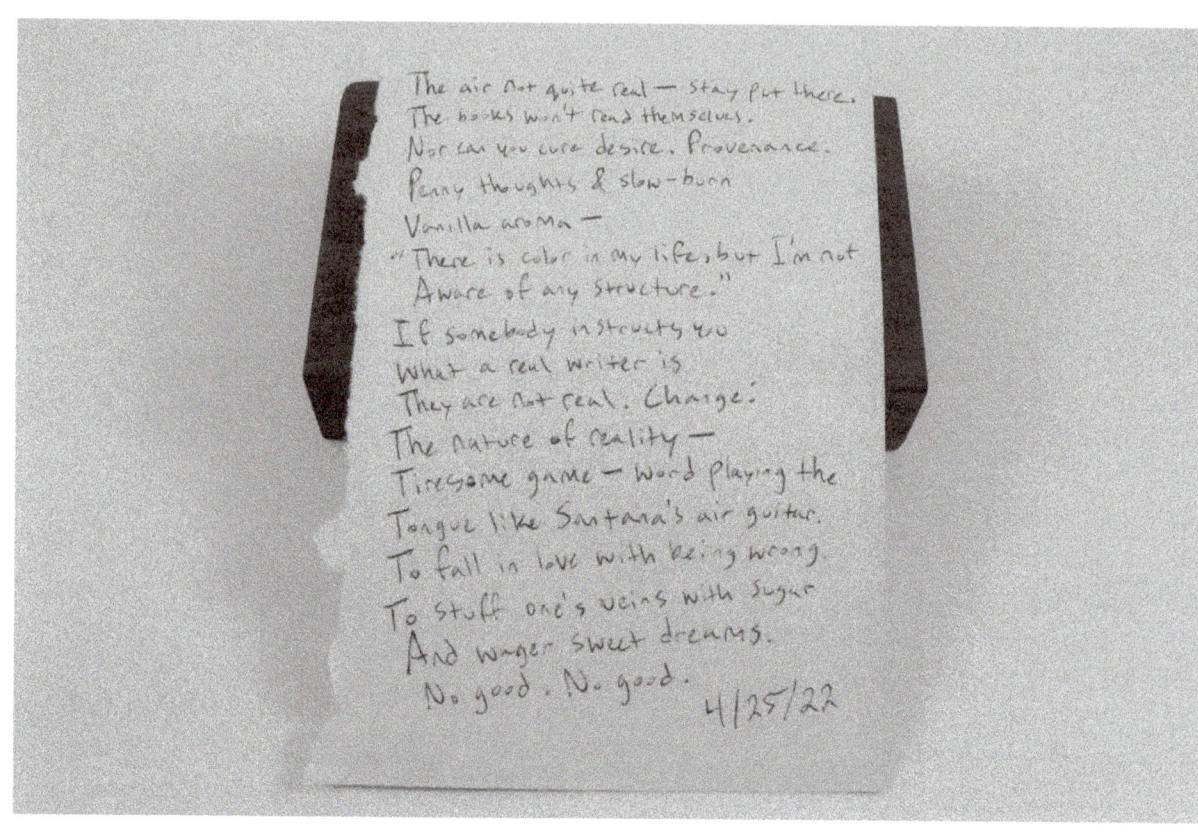

Poem from a leather notepad gifted from one writer to another (pg. 145)

You said to write a poem
About you — so I look into
Your third eye & say
This will have to do —
Has a slice of the ~~universe~~ cosmos
Always been around your
Neck? —
That is my sister,
You say, but this is my
Voice — in some ways
2 big for Texas like every-
One else here — footprints on sand —
There is an art studio
Built on the bones of love
And science, & the artist
Sells her tears — it is 2
Treacherous & beautiful to
Put a price on them — but
The artist must eat — the father
Must be remembered as a dream —
How do you wear the stars around
Your throat? I ask —
They are not for sale, you say,
But I am listening. 4/26/22

Notepad poem (pg. 146)

I.

10 Years ago
I told the story of a girl
Whose bones were
Failing her

And when they did
I couldn't find the story
And since then
The newspaper has yellowed
In a box in my head.

II.

This story really happened
And the girl's family thanked me
And I shot my grief at God
Whose property must be riddled
With bullet holes
In the shape of His imagination.

III.

                    really
The story isn't mine
But she was bald & precious
And wise supposed to say
Thank you, God, for this
Cruel world
In the shape of your imagination?

IV.

Every poem I write
Belongs to me more than
You think
But take them away —

            cannot
I love them
Equally
Which is a sign of a
Good father
With a bad heart
In the shape of
God's Fist —
Revolution is for
Children —
Democracy injured
On the bed of romantics —
Democracy stripped bare
In the waiting room of the
              our dead
Desert where
Await instruction
From a body of light.

V.

This is MY poem —
My life — not my
Life — my story
Finished by you.

Notepad poem No. 2 (pg. 147)

White-napkin poem No. 9 (pg. 149)

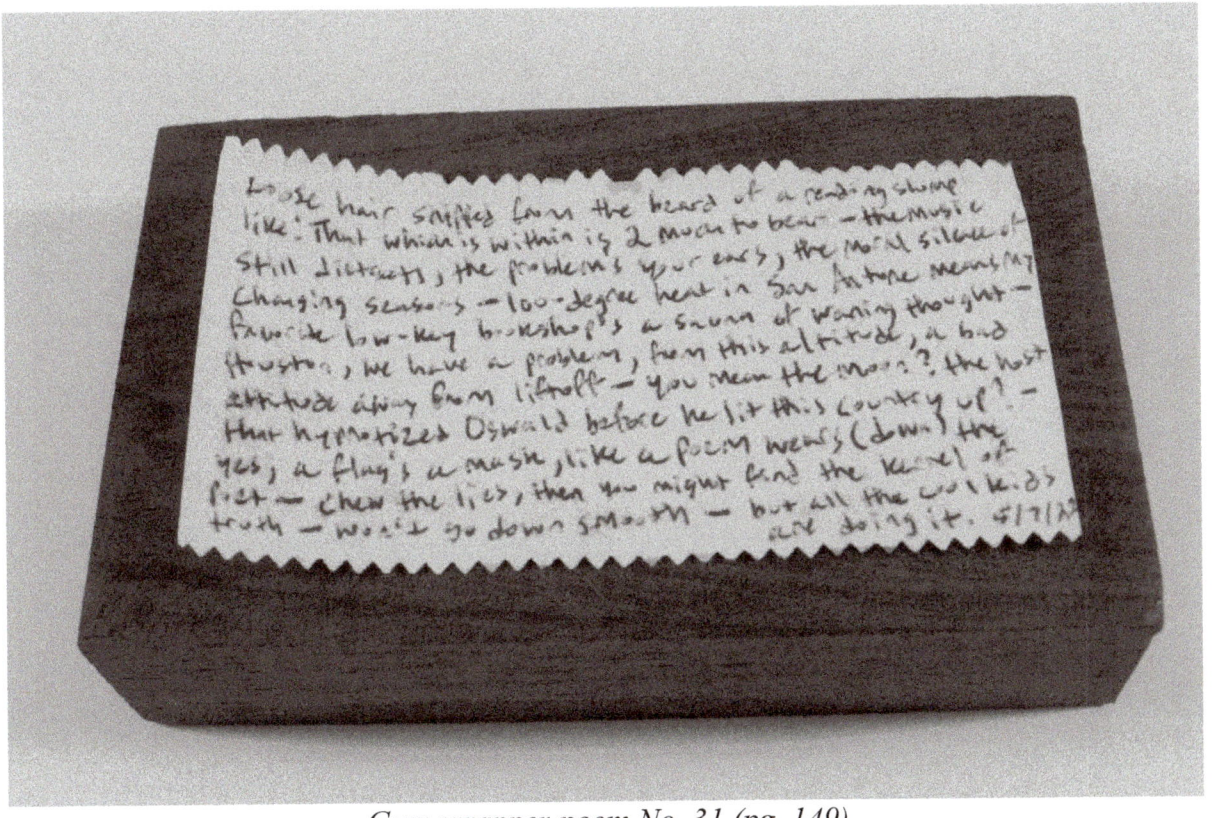

Gum-wrapper poem No. 31 (pg. 149)

Tic Tac poem (pg. 150)

A man in a Ghost face tee
Chaperones his daughter
Dressed in pink to the restroom
And she couldn't be happier,
Not to me, not on this Sunday w/
Temperature & gas prices tearing thru
The record-book roof,
A hole in the soul another kind of
Smiling mouth wrangling its words
Carefully, partner,
For the fabric needs good patchin' —
To my right, Fauci's book titled
Expect the Unexpected —
Yes, the aphorisms will save us,
And when the weather freezes over
In hell
The white coats will wrap us in
White coats &
We'll march down that path single file,
Someone's drum, inner voices,
A child asking her father:
Where are we going, Daddy?
When will we get there?
                              5/15/22

White-napkin poem No. 10 (pg. 150)

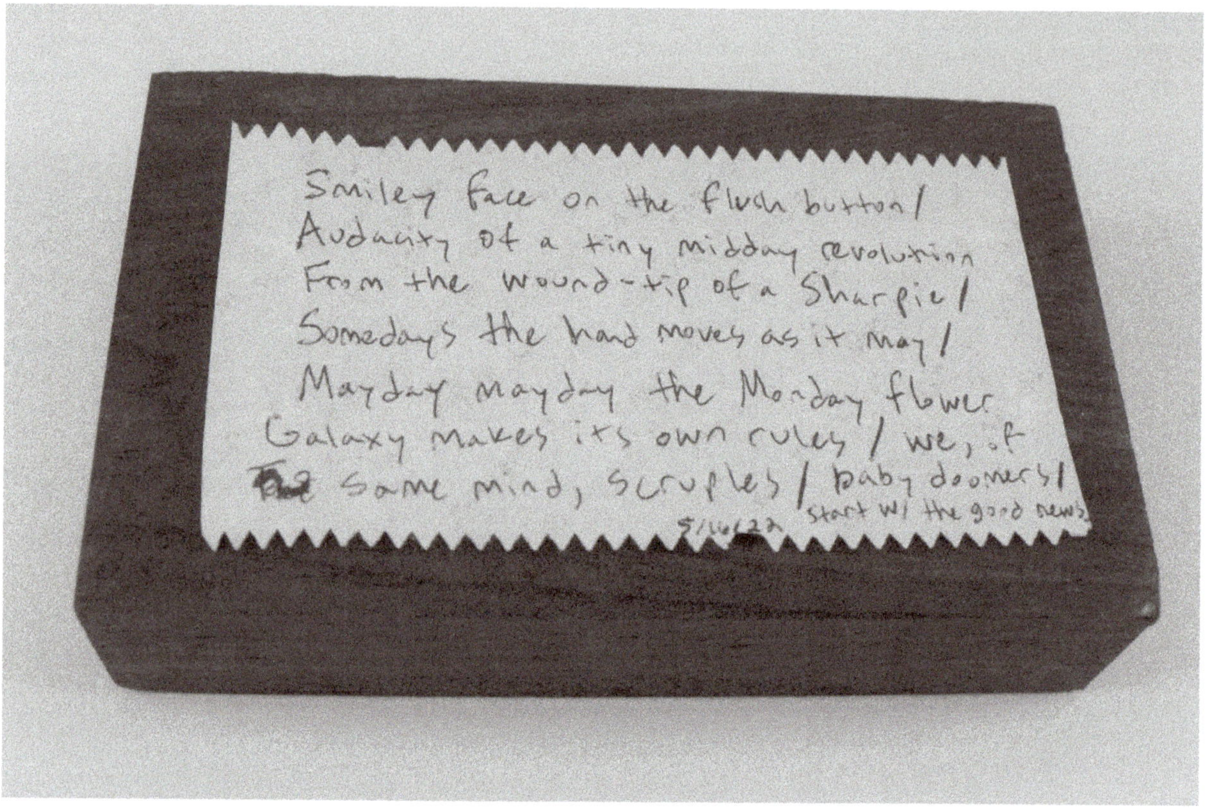

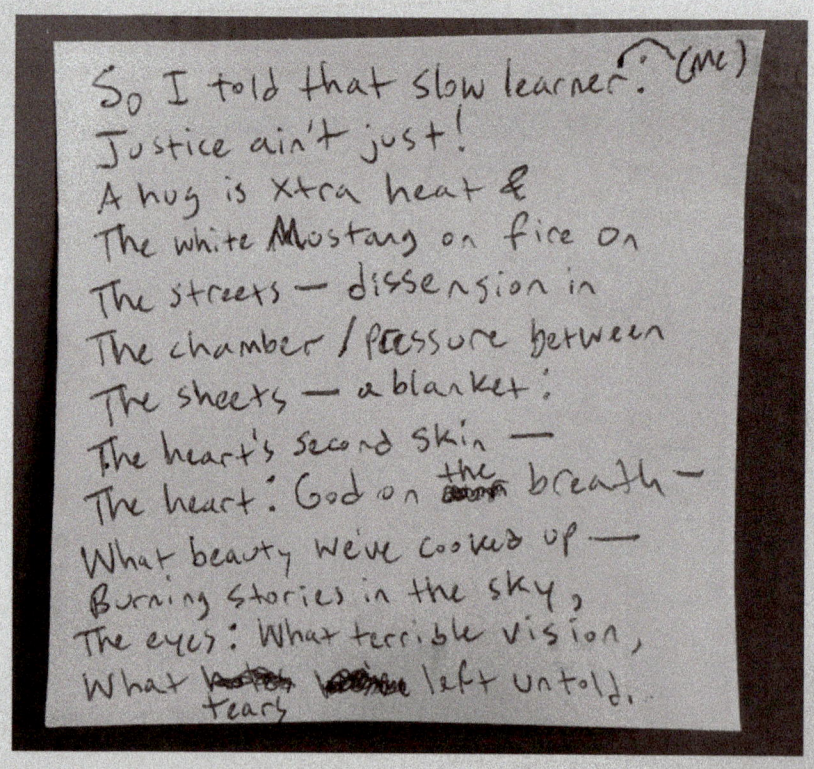

Smiley face on the flush button/
Audacity of a tiny midday revolution
From the wound-tip of a Sharpie/
Somedays the hand moves as it may/
Mayday mayday the Monday flower
Galaxy makes its own rules / we, of
~~The~~ same mind, scruples / baby doomers/
5/16/22 start w/ the good news

Gum-wrapper poem No. 32 (pg. 151)

So I told that slow learner: (MC)
Justice ain't just!
A hug is xtra heat &
The white ~~Mustang~~ Mustang on fire on
The streets — dissension in
The chamber / pressure between
The sheets — a blanket:
The heart's second skin —
The heart: God on ~~the~~ the breath —
What beauty we've cooked up —
Burning stories in the sky,
The eyes: What terrible vision,
What ~~tears~~ ~~tears~~ left untold.
    tears

Post-it Note Poem (pg. 151)

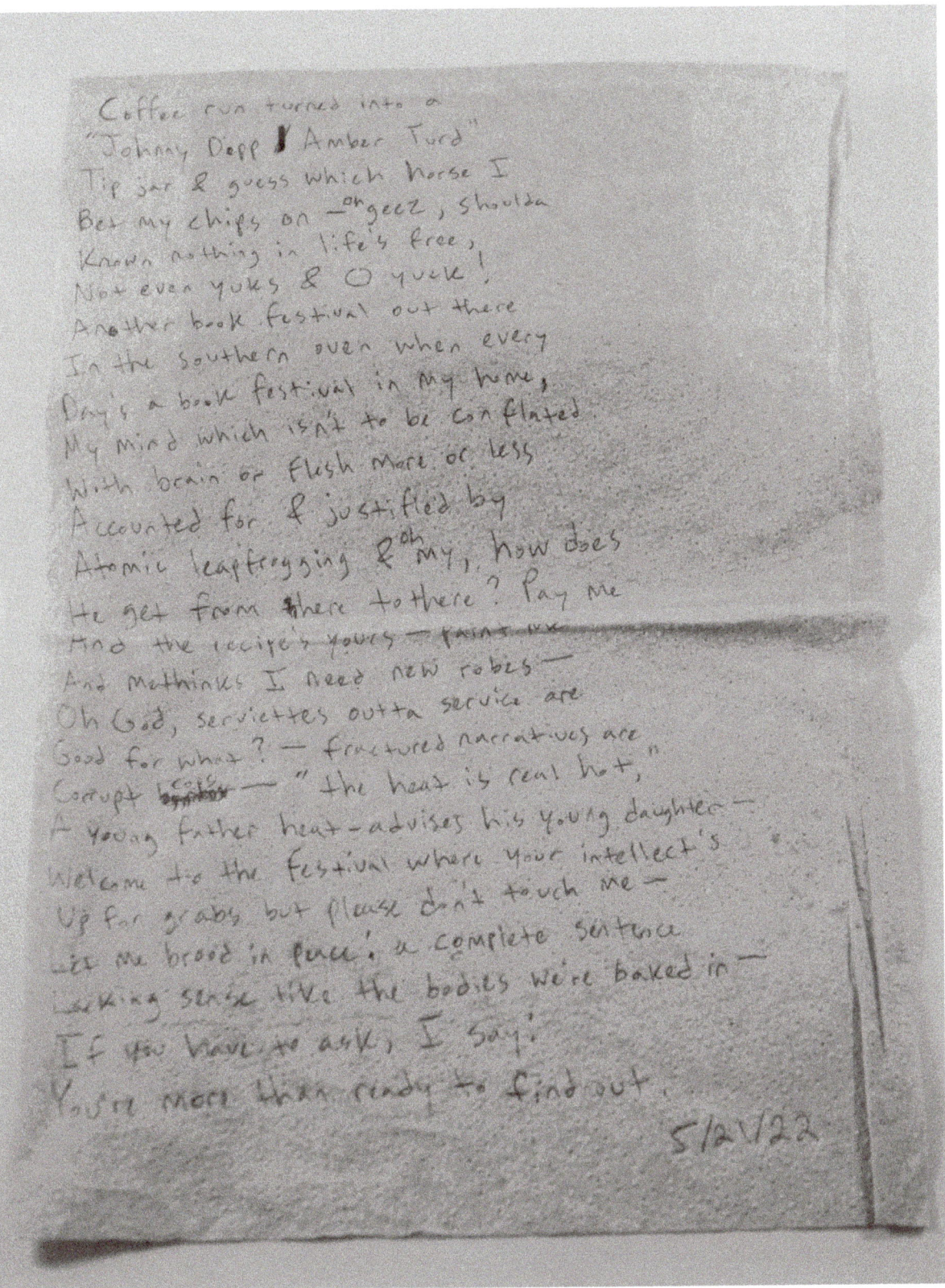

Brown-napkin poem No. 17 (pg. 152)

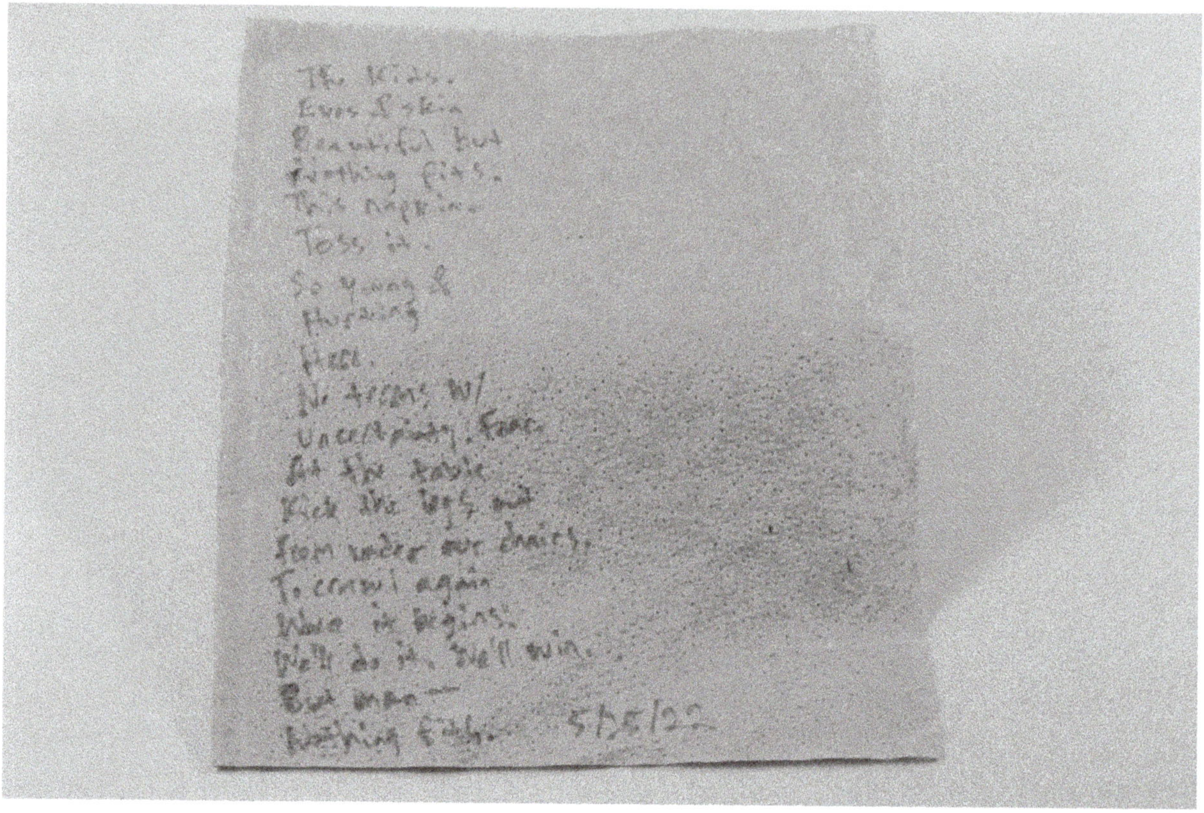

Brown-napkin poem No. 18 (pg. 153)

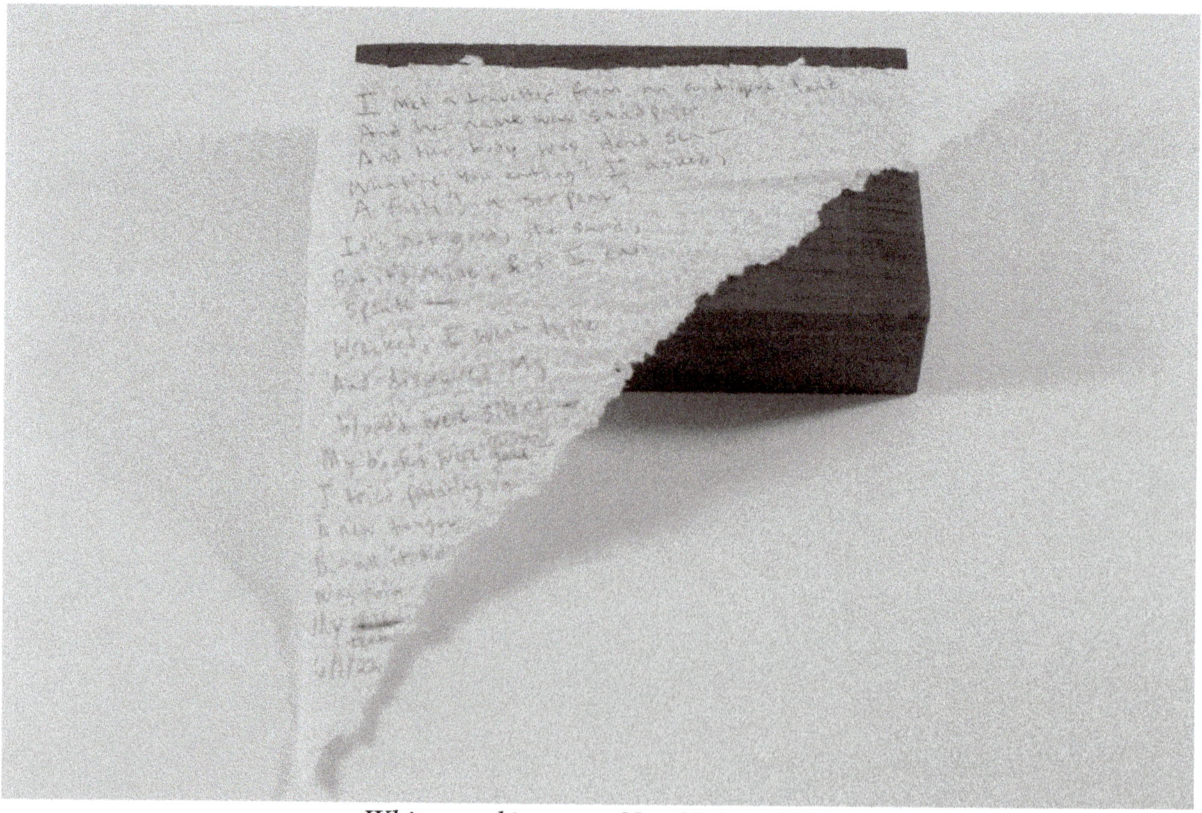

White-napkin poem No. 11 (pg. 153)

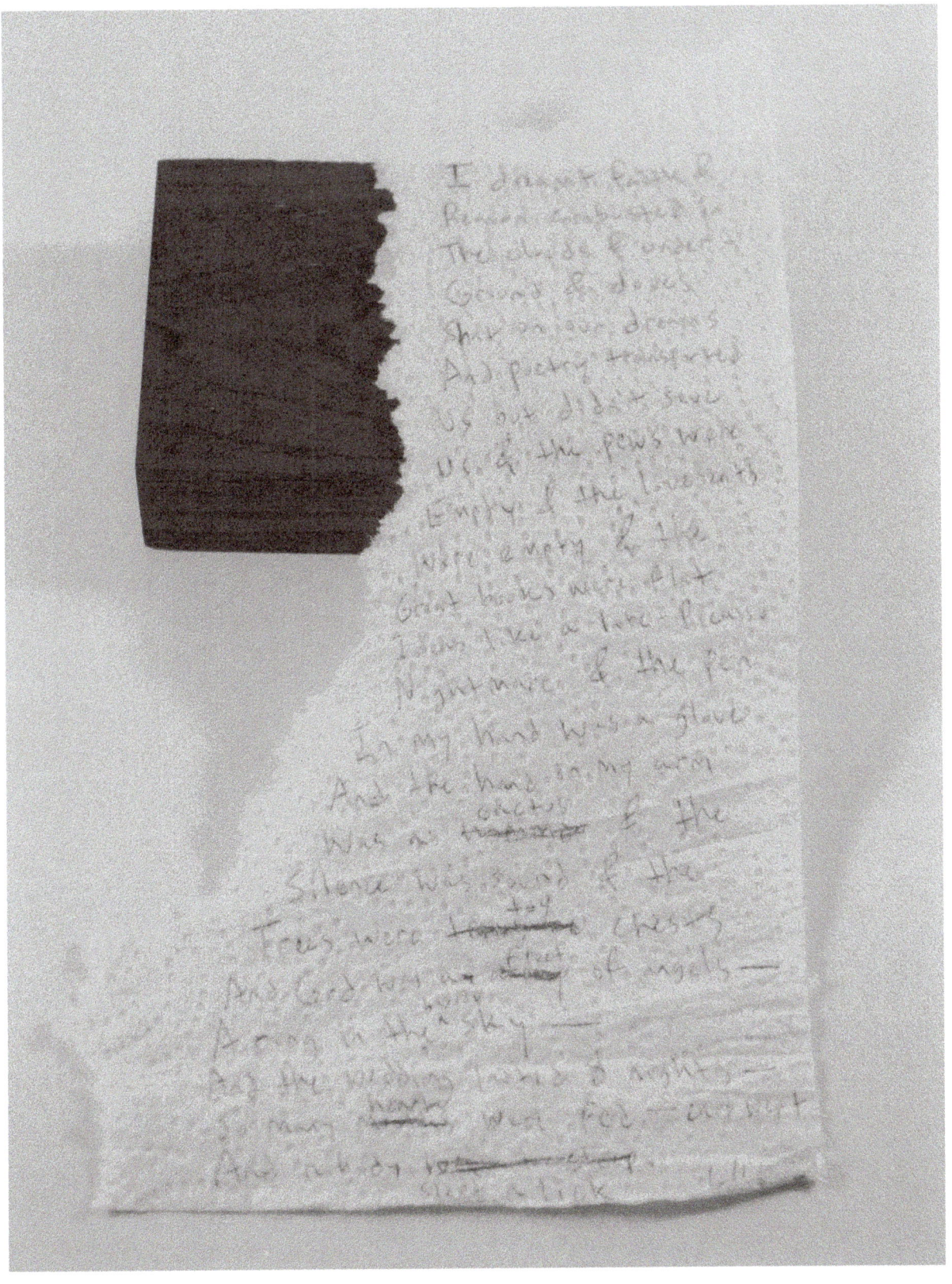

White-napkin poem No. 12 (pg. 154)

I, the past present writing into the future.
What is the future but the past propelled?
What is the present but the future melting
In my ~~palms~~ palms? Is it each of us carrying
3 clocks going up on an escalator
~~Down~~ Down in an elevator
Lying down looking up crushing ~~time~~ time
On our backs — put the I on its side
And the 2 end points signify the beauty, baby,
And horror of parallel inescapability
Which is to say linguistically I am not
Alone — but damn, where'd everybody
Go? It's not that it's lonely at the top
But the birds & lightning are bad at
Telling jokes & when I say "Knock Knock"
I find that it's me on the other side of
The door — there's a ~~home~~ in my hand
In case nobody answers. Planning ahead —
A hydra head of presence. 6/8/22
Knock Knock — I'm already
Home.

White-napkin poem No. 13 (pg. 155)

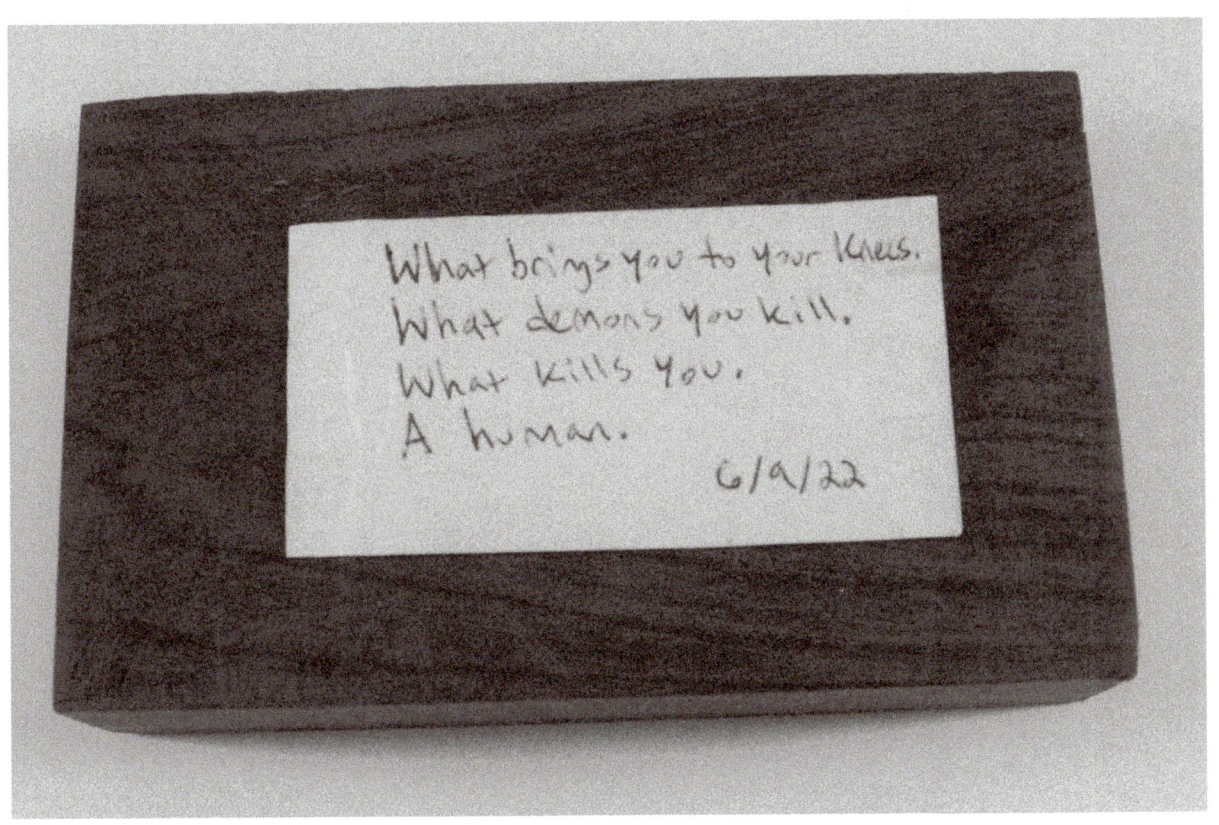

Gum-wrapper poem No. 33 (pg. 155)

I dreamt I was a corn cob pipe dream
And how I developed my tired politics
Slapdash style & hack humor

Was beyond words / just out of reach
Like a duck half a step slow
Like being similar & not even close
Like as not / not as like those
Packed so tight in feelings
Everyplace I (don't) know
Even the desert reeks of tears
Bleeding from all 5 senses like
Mario Santiago Papasquiaro, like
A ~~???~~ homesick child wrecked w/ fear
And where do we go from here?
Mother Teresa said every dream precedes the goal
And that's it, this dream never ends because
Death is temporary & pain is forever
But hey, how about a joke —
A math book slumps into a doctor's office
And grumbles "I've got problems, man" &
Doc says "I see, but I'm only a dentist" —
Even math books carry teeth
You learn something new every day
The sunshine & moonlight in tiny victories
We need only an inch / balled up ~~so~~ so long in armor
I forget how tall you really are
Ain't that something? Hey, ready for another joke?
Just kidding — skidding down the pipe
Our souls on trial scratching the surface of
Trash — the writing is dead

Always has been
Which means we've forgotten
The sin of living in abundance
And if this isn't a poem
Then I'm not a mouth
Biting down hard on my
Heart on fire — my
Tongue be like, "Be cool."
6/14/22

Notepad poem No. 3 (pg. 156)

Water-bottle-cap poem (pg. 157)

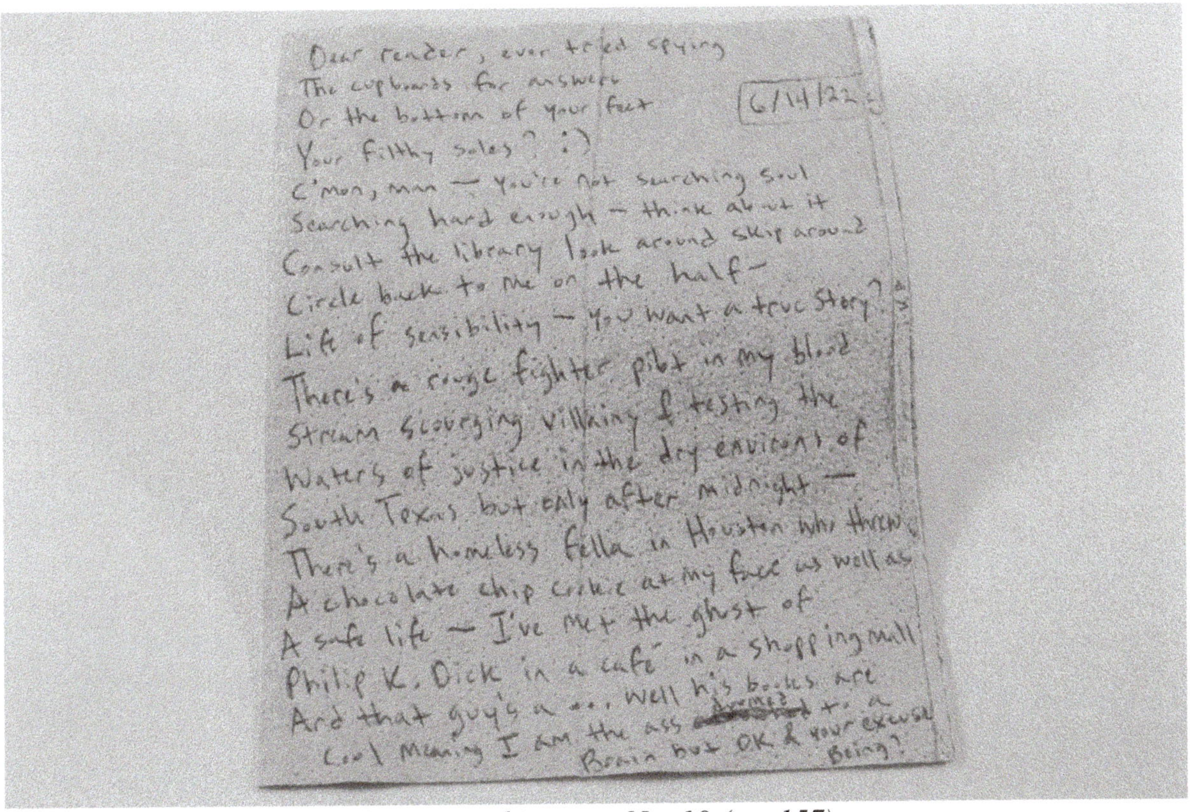

Brown-napkin poem No. 19 (pg. 157)

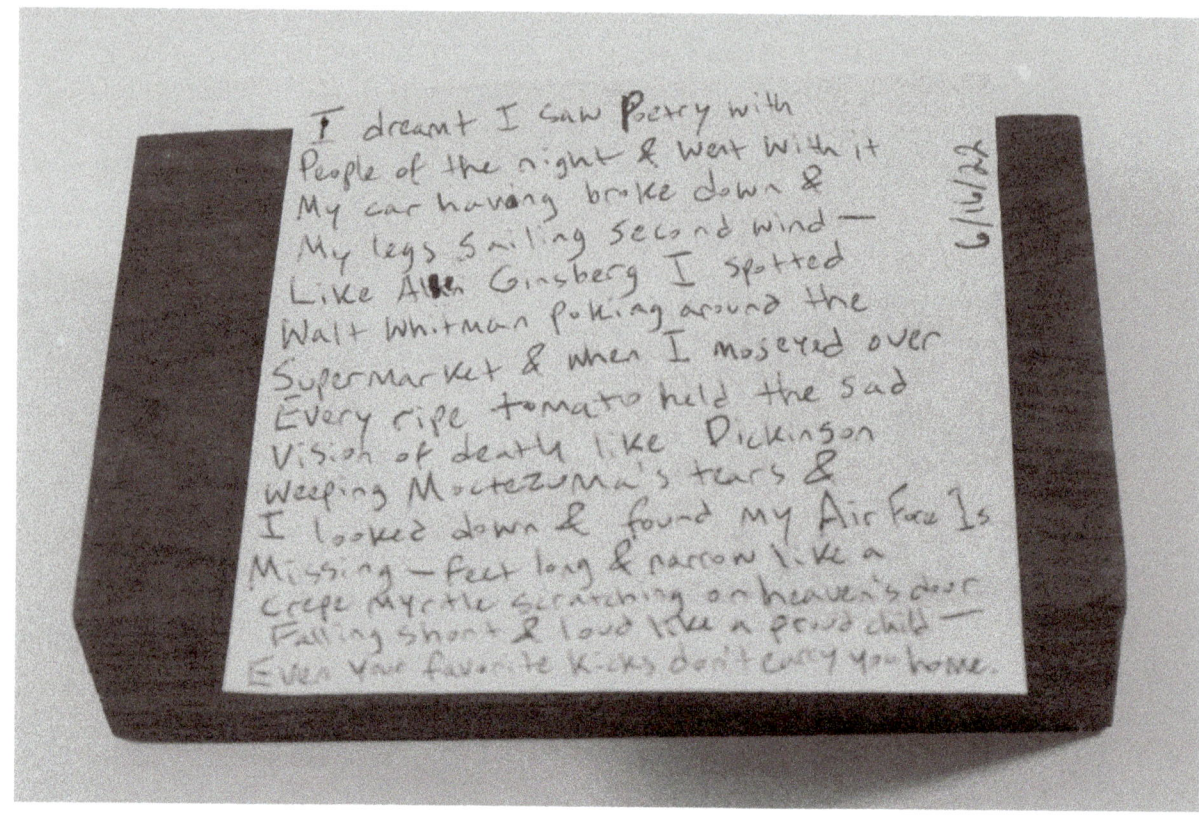

Post-it Note poem No. 2 (pg. 158)

Paper-towel poem (pg. 159)

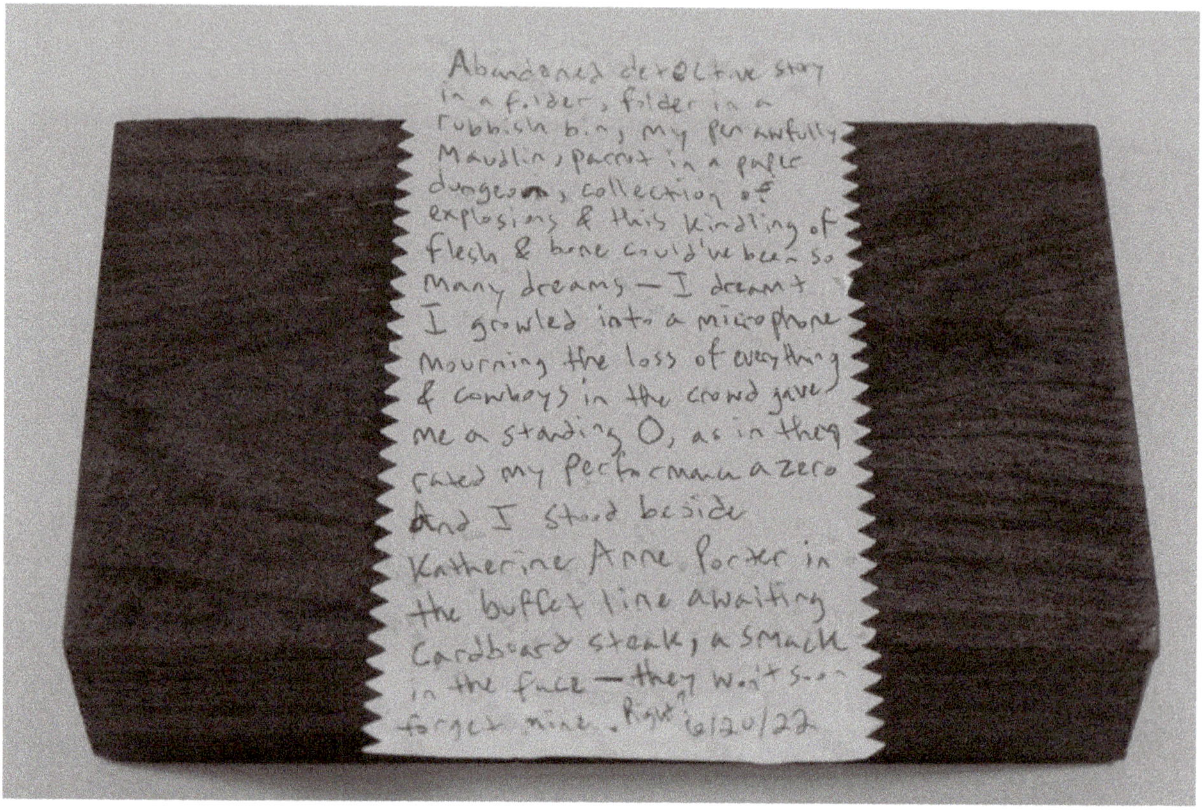

Abandoned detective story in a folder, folder in a rubbish bin, my pen awfully maudlin, parrot in a paper dungeon, collection of explosions & this kindling of flesh & bone could've been so many dreams — I dreamt I growled into a microphone mourning the loss of everything & cowboys in the crowd gave me a standing O, as in they rated my performance a zero and I stood beside Katherine Anne Porter in the buffet line awaiting cardboard steak, a smack in the face — they won't soon forget mine. Rgk 6/20/22

Gum-wrapper poem No. 34 (pg. 160)

Nothing to cling to Ashes, three homes — no will. Hey Papa, you laughing? 6/21/22

Gum-wrapper haiku (pg. 160)

Bookmark haiku (pg. 161)

I dreamt I was approaching the end of the dream—
33 steps in, long but soon forgotten like years, My
Father's eyes, my mother's smile (& ears), Grand-
Father's legs and Grandma's cast-iron will pushing me
Past weeds and beach shells cutting my heels,
The host isn't nice but it's right, I see the writing in
The sky, that blue ghost I know, beautiful stars
Around it's neck, Vonnegut's words in my grief,
You've gotta fling that death wish out there, someone's
Chambers, someone's waiting room, the beds are all
Lying to you, the dream's almost there, Tumbleweed Drive
To tumbleweed sprint across the plains of delivery
And graves, the water lapping at your feet, the
Woods nice but not right, they're mine & yours,
Inching toward the illusion of a great dividing line—
I dreamt I approached the end of the dream &
My pages trailed behind like neglected offspring
And someday they'd make me pay, but not yet, today,
Heroes letting me down & I retelling their tales of
Nightmares and runaway lovers, we should've seized
The lights, it's not too late, right, t. fall down &
Grow up again? the dream is ending but I hold back
These tears, I'm listening, my pen is ready — yes,
Happy to scratch fresh legends into the dirt, the
Harvest, the earth your heart brushing against my
Cheeks a million birthday wishes — a soft kiss
For each — that those comes true.

6/23/22

Page-ripped-from-a-book poem (pg. 161)

Heat dome—
You should see my finances, tho!
Only the necessities, bank stacks
Growing to the ceiling... Oh/high, Jack
"God, why didn't they close her eyes?"
Remarked my Mom upon seeing Frida's
Black-n-white corpse at the end of the
Painful documentary — she's told me time
And again she doesn't want to burden
Us — & then she shows me old
Family photos — beautiful and painful —
My mind isn't w/ this poem but somewhere
In Italy, dreaming in a Spanish tongue
Lost — a thunderstorm won't stop
The heat to come — is love present or is it
Already gone

Brown-napkin poem No. 20 (pg. 162)

On this 6th day of September 2022,
$2.55 burrowing its way to my wallet
(Poetry royalties)
I rest here unregal
Supremely regaled by 2 dead white authors
In my bone-dry Vise-grip
Pondering dead words left
Inside the tank
And how anyone cares about anything—
2 am out; oh! the baton twirlers
In a kind of beautiful living hell
And try as I might to hopscotch galaxies
I awake to the same dream
Return to the same red smile (lovely)
Filling my half-gone Pixie cup w/ water
For I am thirsty and thrive in a circular
Garden filled w/ infinite ideas & windows &
The promise of tomorrow—
A gleam in your green underground eyes—
It speaks in your tongue &
It was home long before you arrived

White-napkin poem No. 14 (pg. 162)

Coffee-sleeve poem No. 8 (pg. 163)

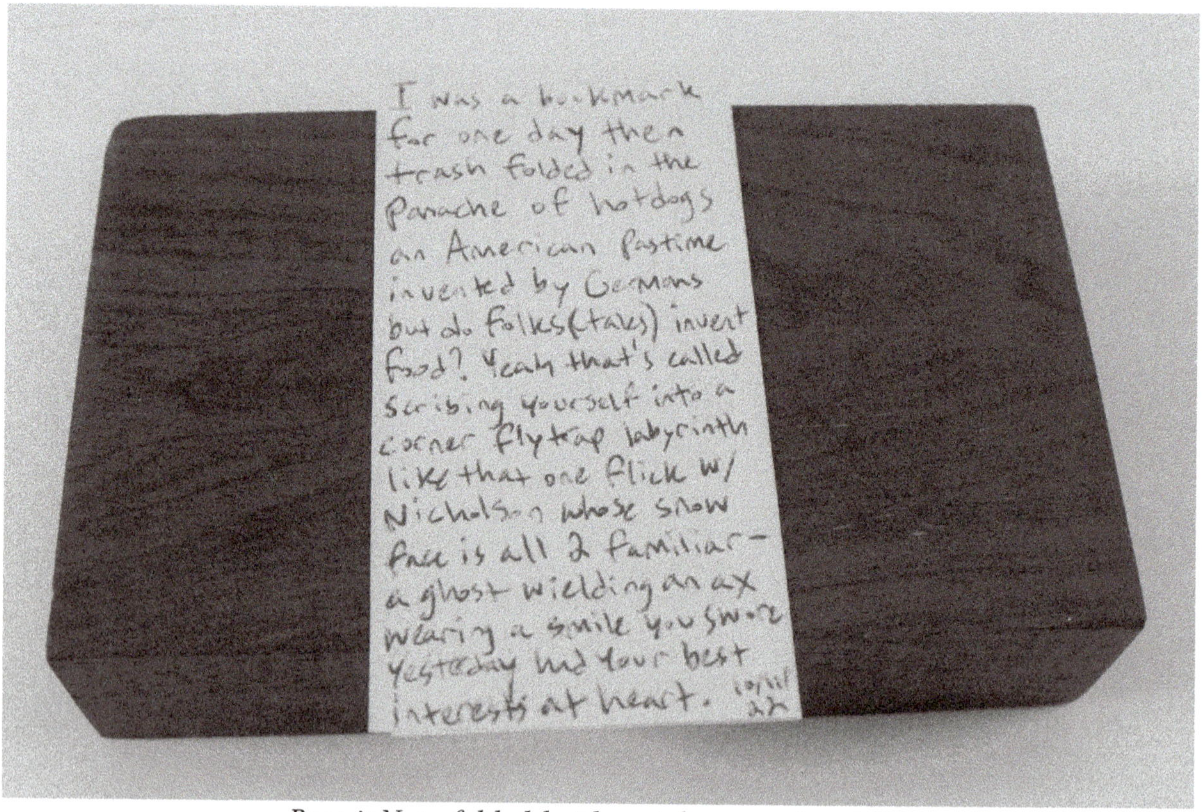

Post-it Note-folded-hotdog-style-poem (pg. 163)

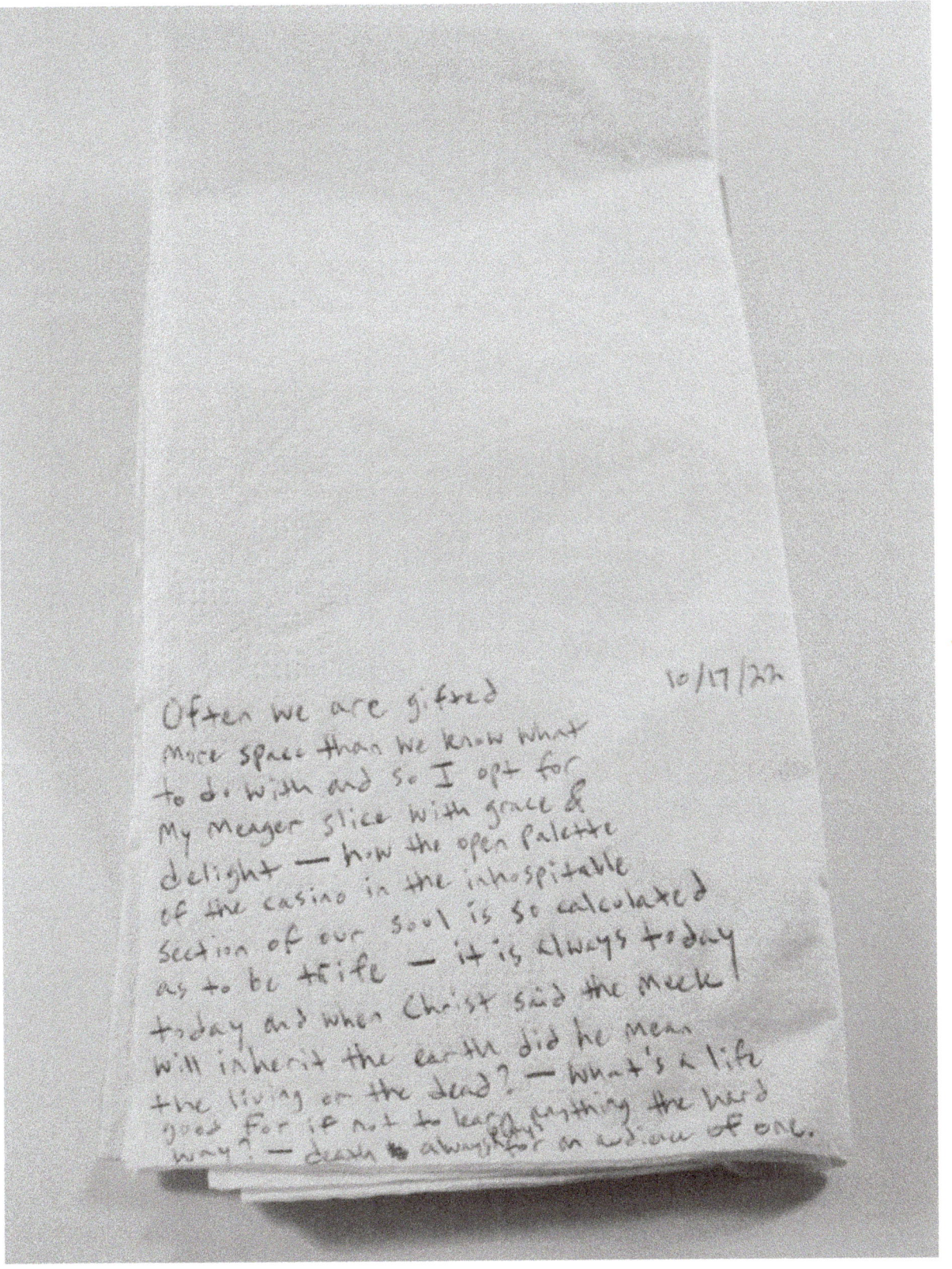

White-napkin poem No. 15 (pg. 164)

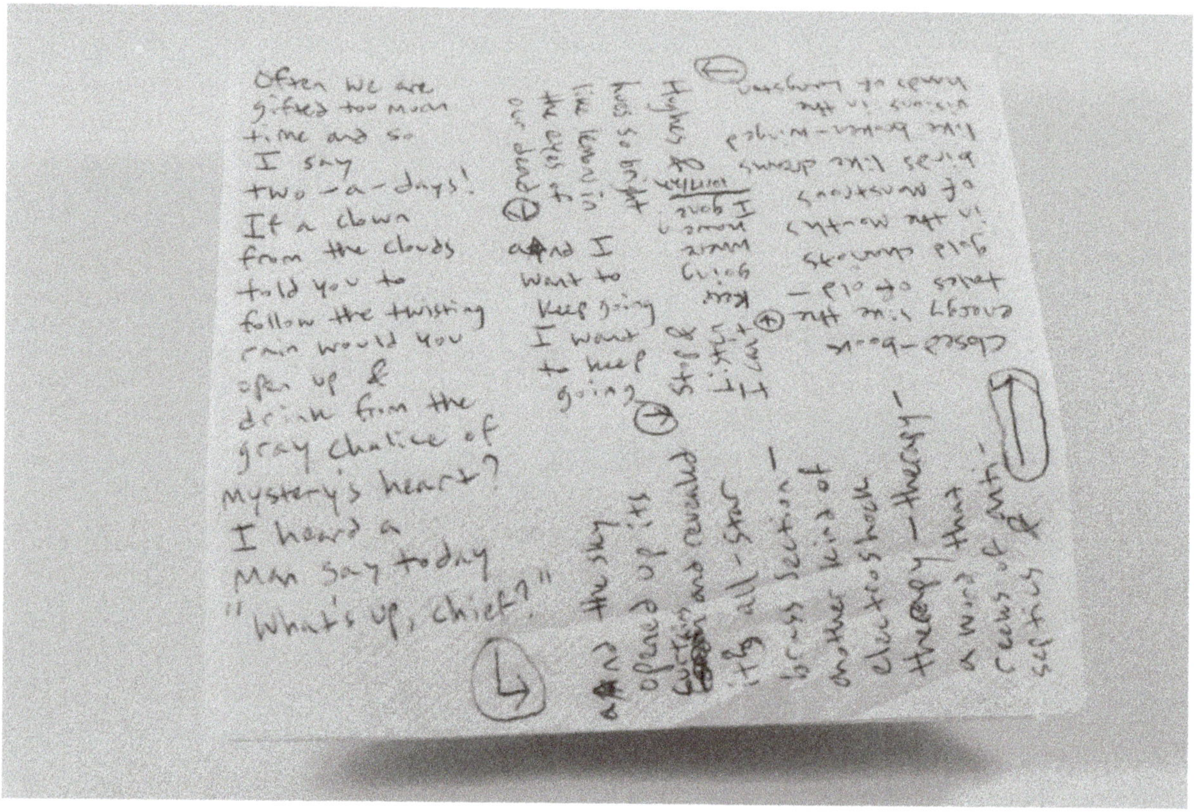

White-napkin poem No. 16 (pg. 165)

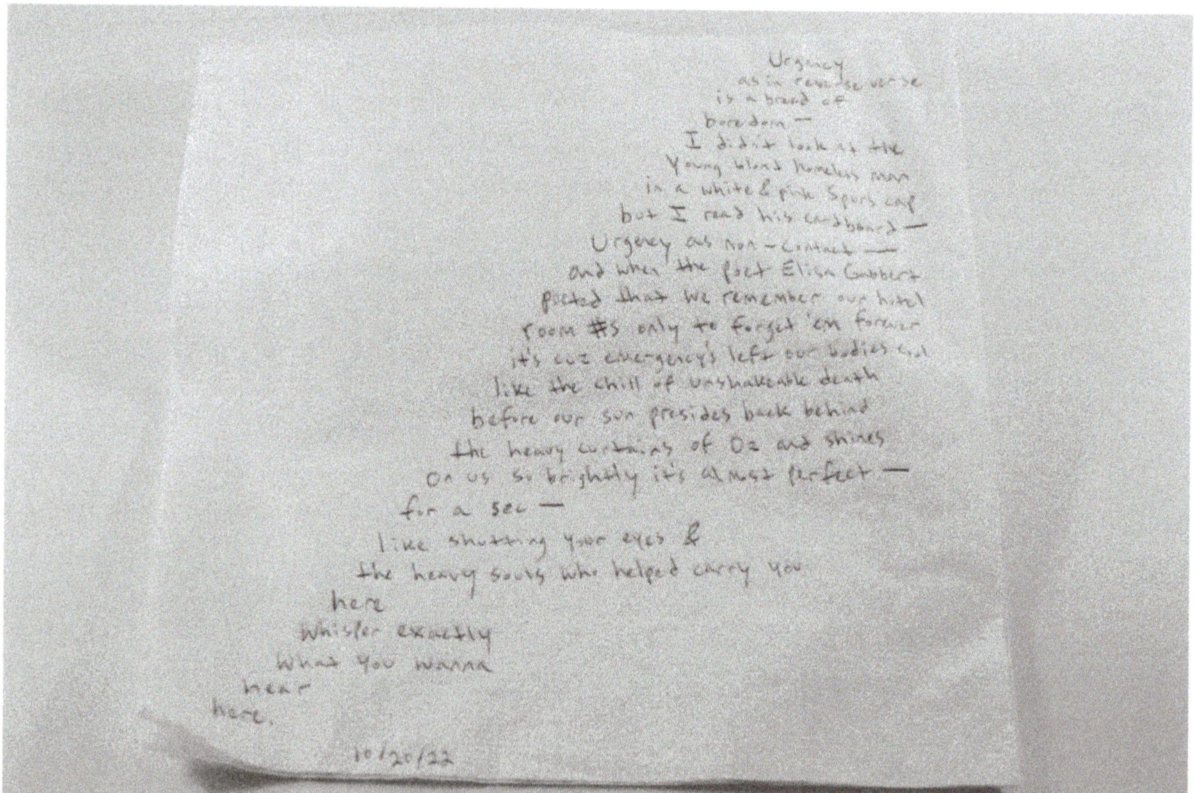

White-napkin poem No. 17. (pg.166)

McDonald's coffee-cup poem No. 2 (pg. 167)

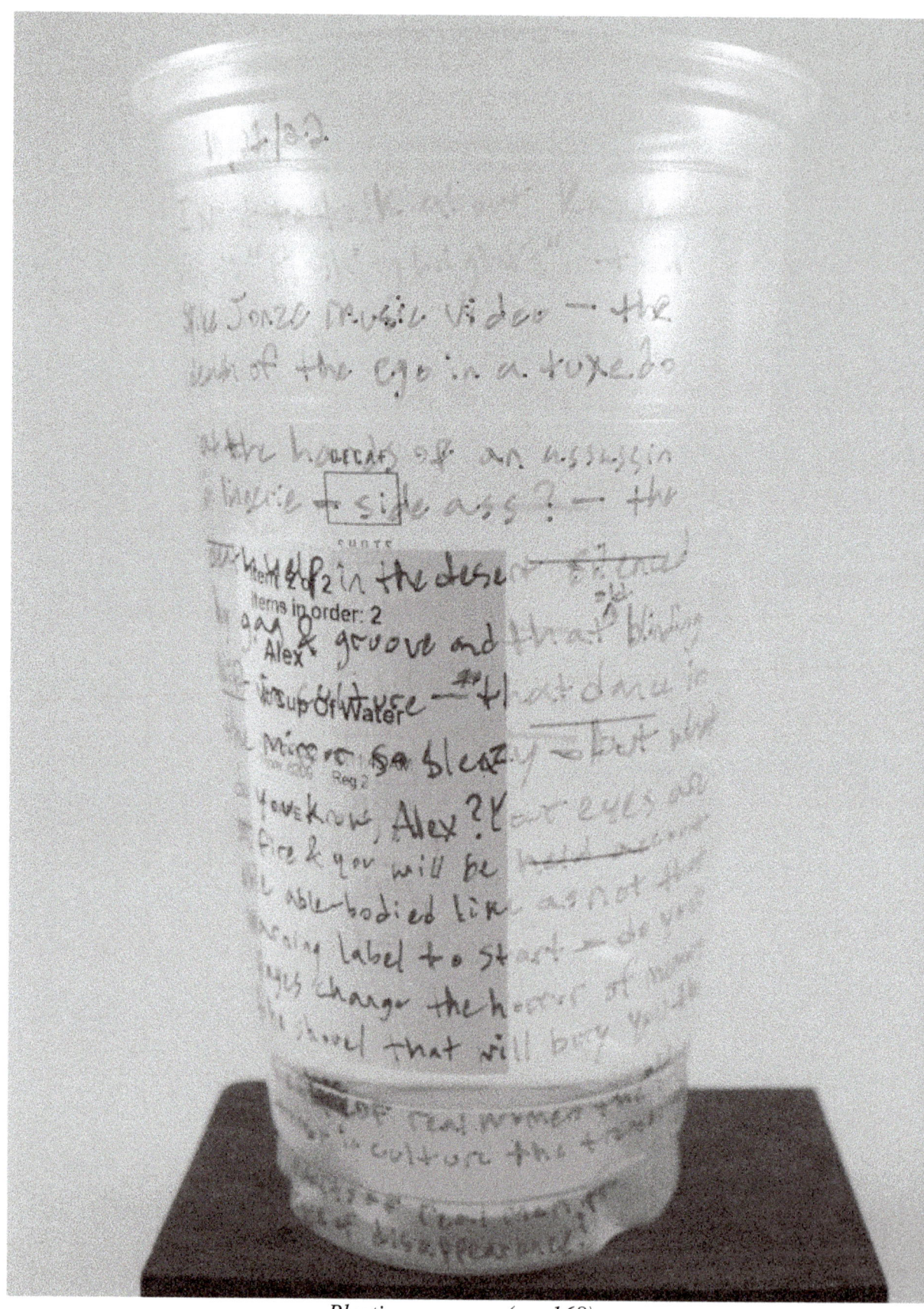

Plastic-cup poem (pg. 168)

I wanna talk a lil' more bout   10/23/22
Ye's "Flashing Lights" cuz I wasn't
done (space restrictions) and I am the
eye on fire behind the white curtain
sunglasses ~~the~~ reviving always dying &
always ~~conjuring~~ like the Terminator —
yes, the killer behind the ~~fake~~ flesh as I am
the soul behind the cold prose & West the hot
note behind the man behind the ~~dark~~ monster
endless night — O how many times I've
heard friends recite ~~say~~ "Fuck Kanye" and I'm
like, Hey, some attacks are personal
but all are vital — hey, are we all not
merging into that abyss day by ~~night?~~
Salinas, could it be ~~that~~ you're showing off
(I never thought you would take it this far)
but this ain't nothing they don't ~~already~~ know —
is theater of ... cruelty everything is ... base & shock & shadow.

White-napkin poem No. 18 (pg. 168)

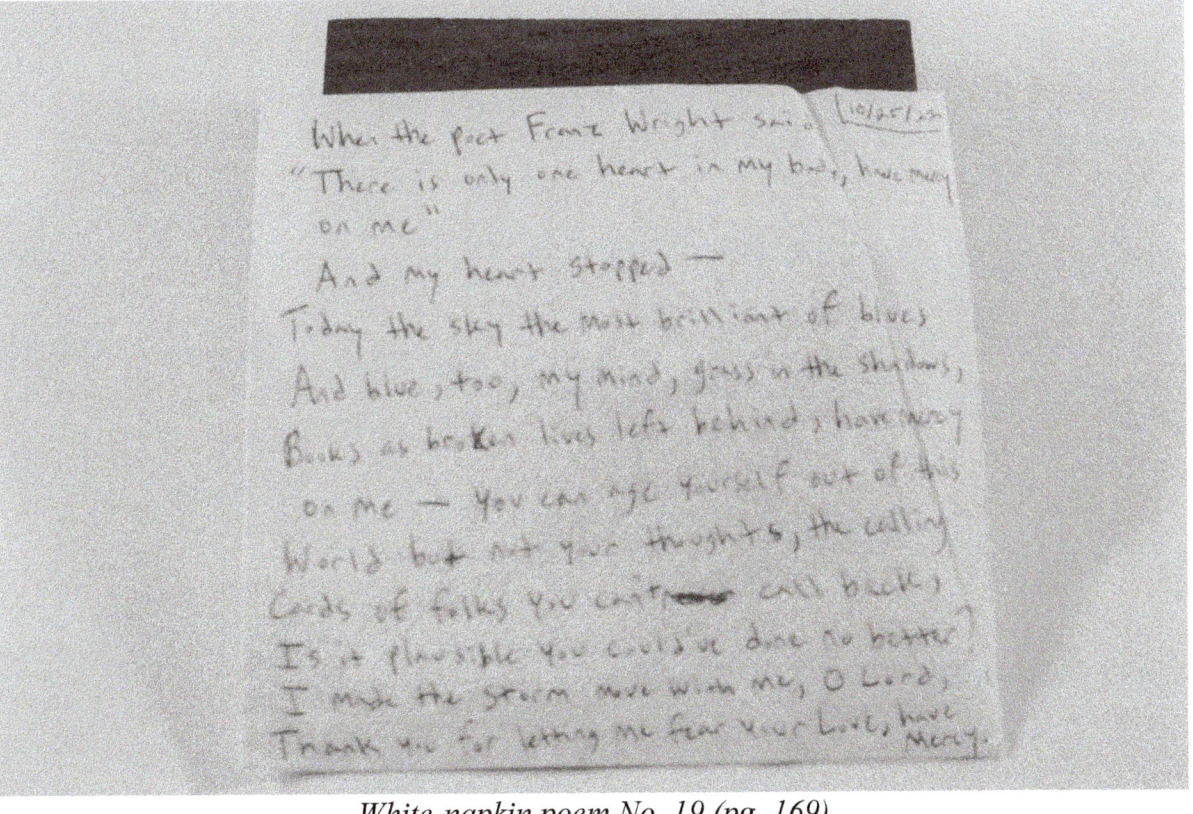

When the poet Franz Wright said
"There is only one heart in my body, have mercy
on me"
And my heart stopped —
Today the sky the most brilliant of blues
And blue, too, my mind, grass in the shadows,
Books as broken lives left behind, have mercy
on me — You can age yourself out of this
world but not your thoughts, the calling
cards of folks you can't ~~ever~~ call back,
Is it plausible you could've done no better?
I make the storm move with me, O Lord,
Thank you for letting me fear your Love, have
Mercy.

White-napkin poem No. 19 (pg. 169)

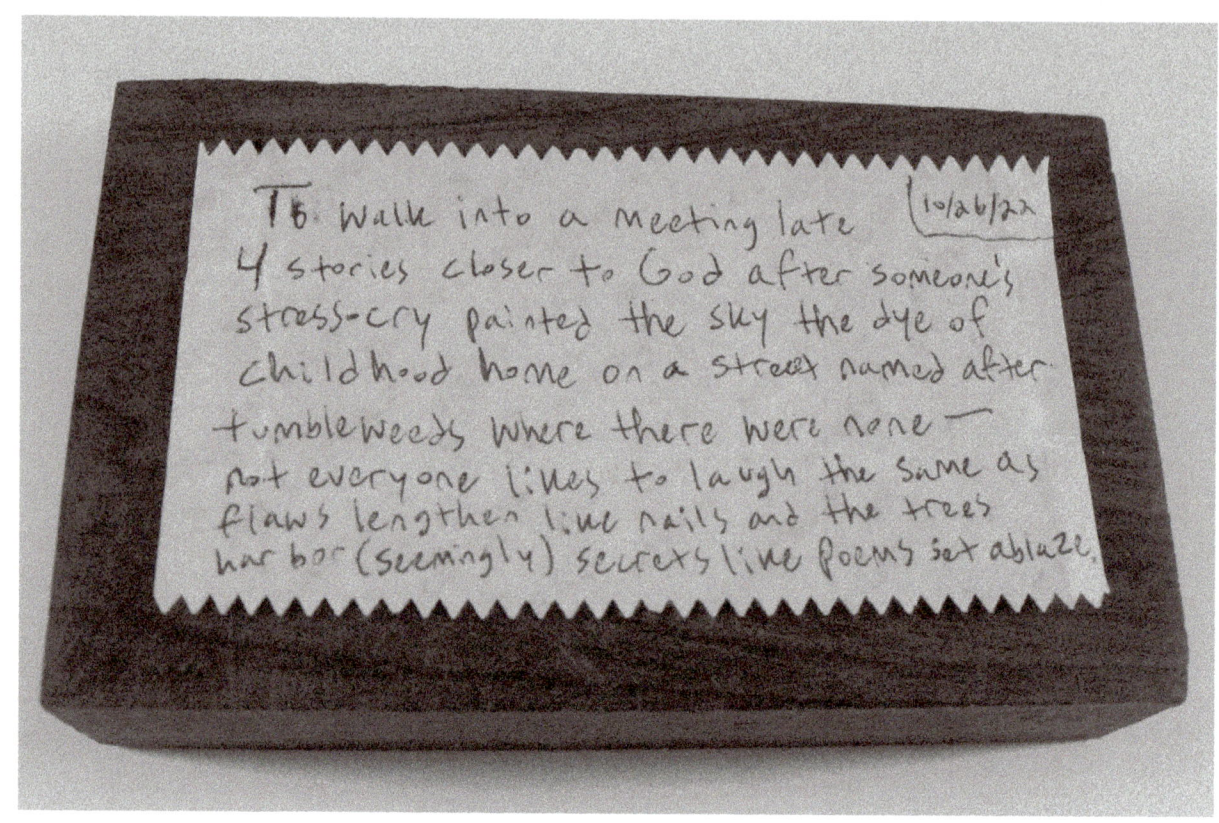

Gum-wrapper poem No. 35 (pg. 169)

That's it — it's taken me 20
white napkins to understand
again
the perfect poem does not exist
here
because it lives (for now) in our hearts
(unwritten) only for us
to survive
and so this insane chase must ensue —
but damn
the illusive motions have meant
so much
like a simple flip of the red hair,
your scent on me in the cinema
dark till the end of dreams
which I misplace again &
again
and so the chase resurrected
under the watch of dying stars
and the "I" trying so hard to leave
its body behind like a foolish monk
with iron fists or the crucifix
buried in a drawer —
force majeure —
I don't wanna chase you anymore
but off the page you flee into the green
so what am I supposed to do,
sit here and think?   10/27/22

White-napkin poem No. 20 (pg. 170)

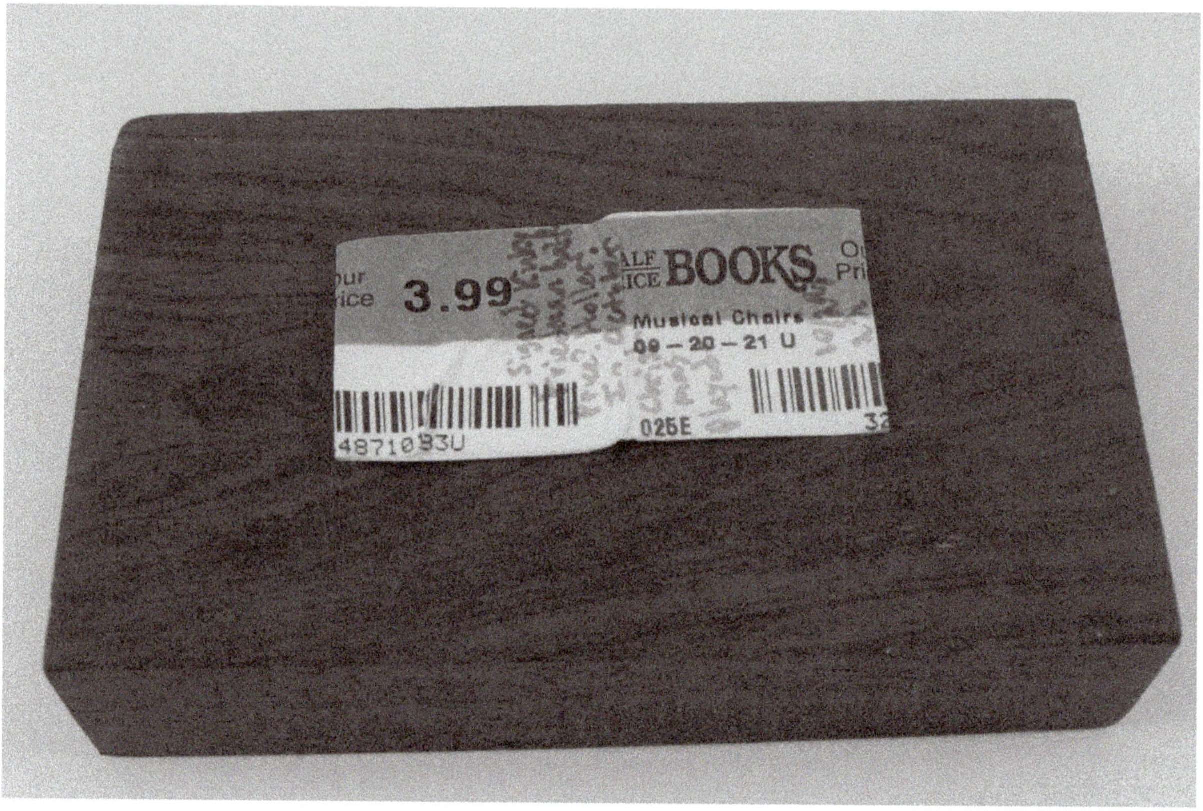

Half Price Books price-tag haiku (pg. 170)

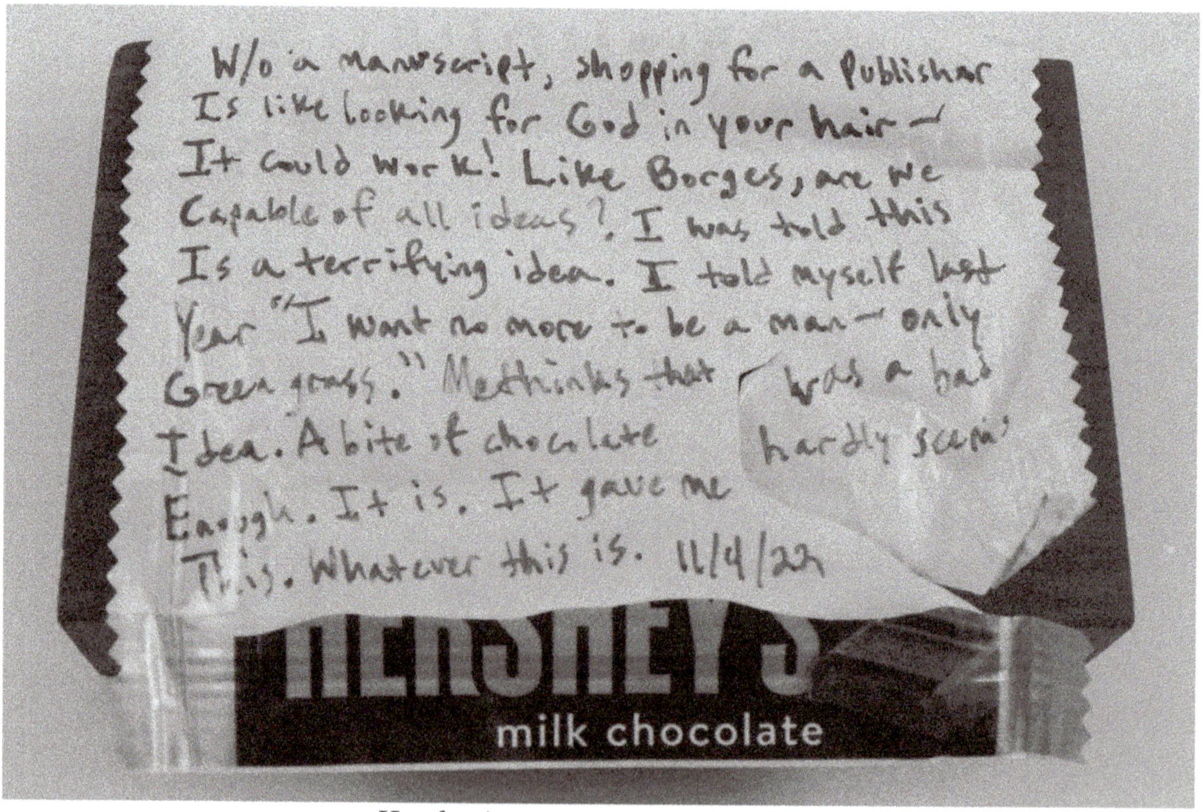

W/o a manuscript, shopping for a publisher
Is like looking for God in your hair —
It could work! Like Borges, are we
capable of all ideas? I was told this
Is a terrifying idea. I told myself last
Year "I want no more to be a man — only
Green grass." Methinks that was a bad
Idea. A bite of chocolate hardly seems
Enough. It is. It gave me
This. Whatever this is. 11/4/22

HERSHEY'S
milk chocolate

Hershey's wrapper poem (pg. 171)

Gum-wrapper poem No. 36 (pg. 171)

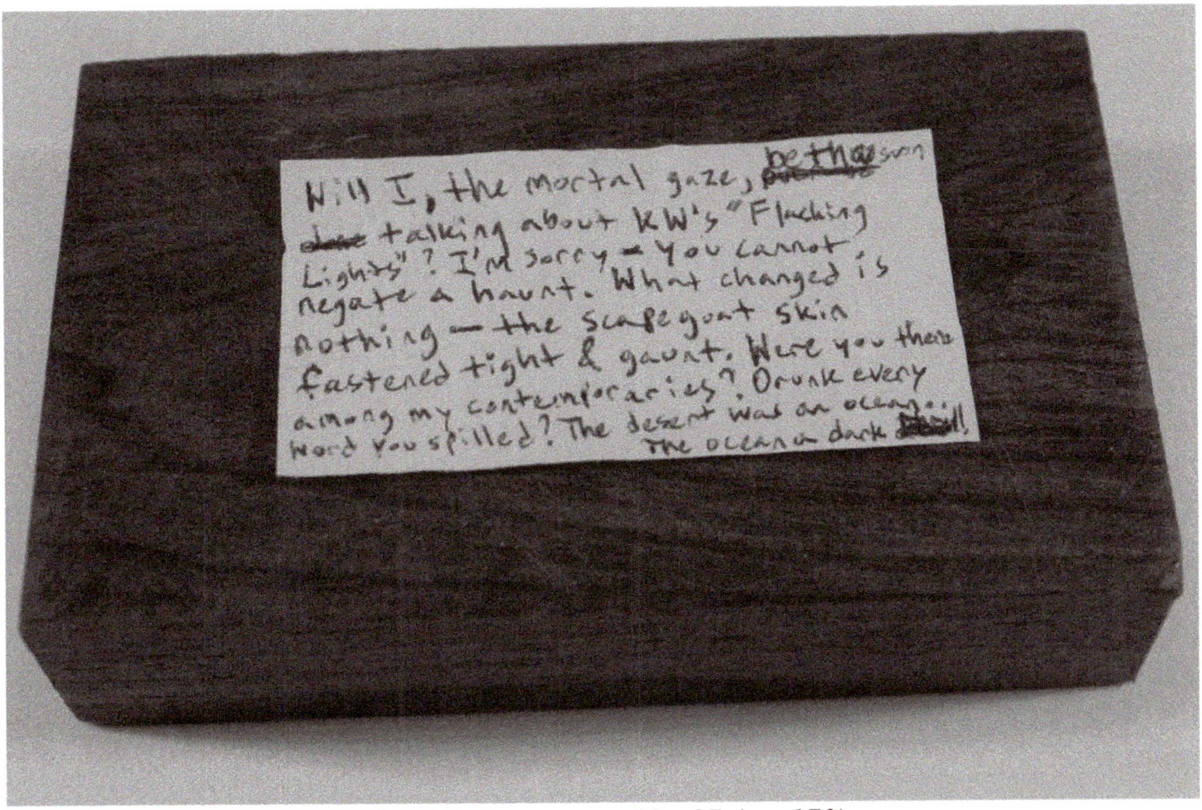

Gum-wrapper poem No. 37 (pg. 172)

Coffee-lid poem (pg. 172)

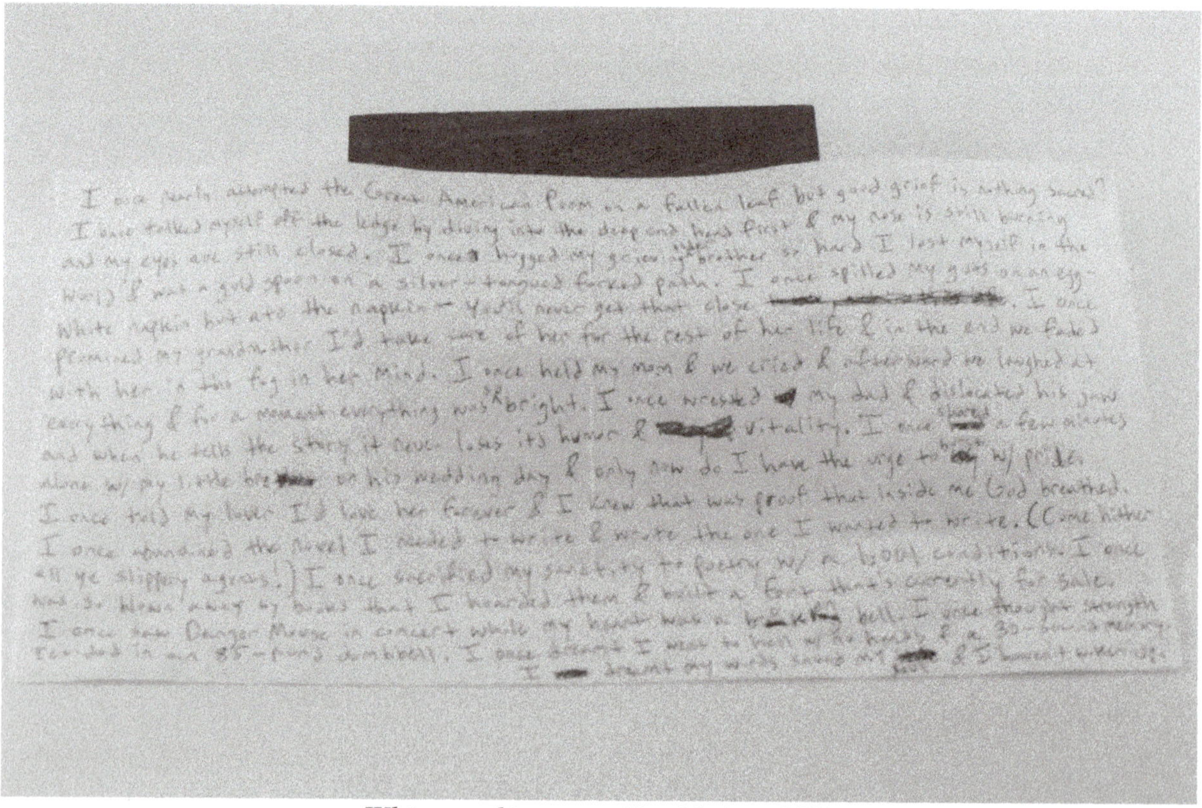

White-napkin poem No. 21 (pg. 173)

Google Partners

This is not an endoresment — it's self-inflicted tunnel vision. God, how some books are on fire. We were driving down Wurzbach during the witching hour when she said James Cain's The Postman Always Rings Twice was written in gasoline. I said, "Yes, and nothing is left of that world." I have secrets not even Death will pry out of me. I ~~grabbed~~ seized this pen only because my nerve endings tingled — the shark is swimming thru my ~~heart~~. The difference between prose & poetry is the brash moon or the shy host on the Black Spandex. I was born to die in myself. I live to exhaust extant ink under my feet which do not always carry me home. I own the words that own me. The letdown is that people fill in their ghosts like Magritte's Pilgrim. The letdown is that legends are boiled into words. (This is a good problem to have.) Some of my gasoline lives in a Nike shoebox; I wear a 10 when I'm not ~~fleeing~~ from my life. The last night of the Earth means it's still night. Whether you die or not, always hit 'em with "Cool invite." When Frida said, "I hope the exit is joyful," & left us w/ her appetite. I'm here for it, I am part blind but my wings work just fine. Coming! Alright.

Notepad poem No. 4 (pg. 174)

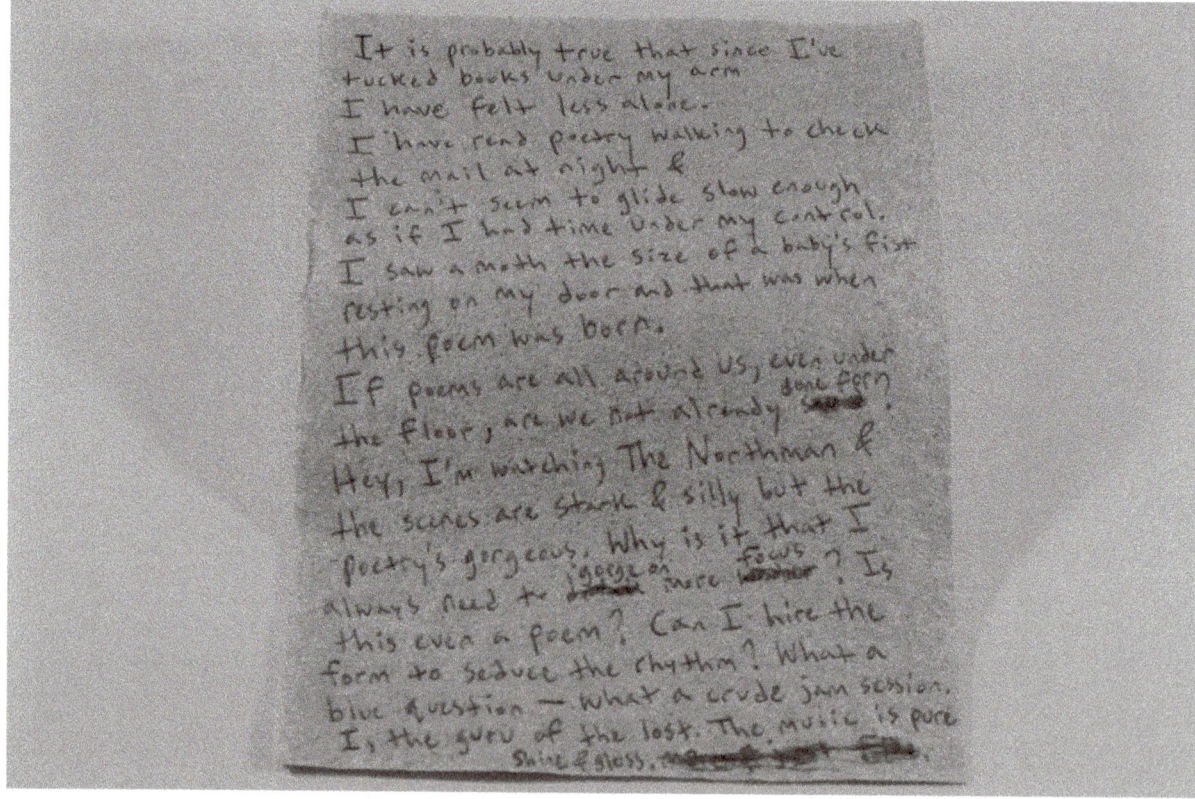

Water-lid poem (pg. 175)

Brown-napkin poem No. 21 (pg. 175)

Brown-napkin poem No. 22 (pg. 176)

This BIC Atlantis has dragged one places, man.
Nestled me & shut the blinds — (oh, it's
that kinda date?) — skirted my 3rd eye
(the only vision that binds) straight from the
grave of Georges Bataille — flicked the lights
off & on & yes — time for the final taste on
Ye's "Flashing Lights" — how there are 2 many
star (killers) to count & the Night (that
journey) & the frigid rule — I worry & hurt
for you — seen this show peering up from the
bottom of the blackbottom pool — (attached to
the mermaid, guide me home, Missile Muse) —
there's nowhere as far as the dark gallery of
your heart — let me in — waltz me out — in
my mouth a pilfered meteorite — slash in the
fan — the desert's soul — antique rug buried in
the billionth hole —
rigged rigamarole of burnt bridges — song
on repeat till I perish or cherish the Angel
of Death — a "Powered by Bitchdust"
bumper sticker on the old pickup truck —
I don't suppose you're 3 handfuls
of double trouble? — chief
chieftain Robert Parish swingin'
for the win — the good green
westward grin full of
heaven & sin — spin
this venom — wire of
blood thru the
chin.
Water

White-napkin poem No. 22 (pg. 177)

80 | Trash Poems

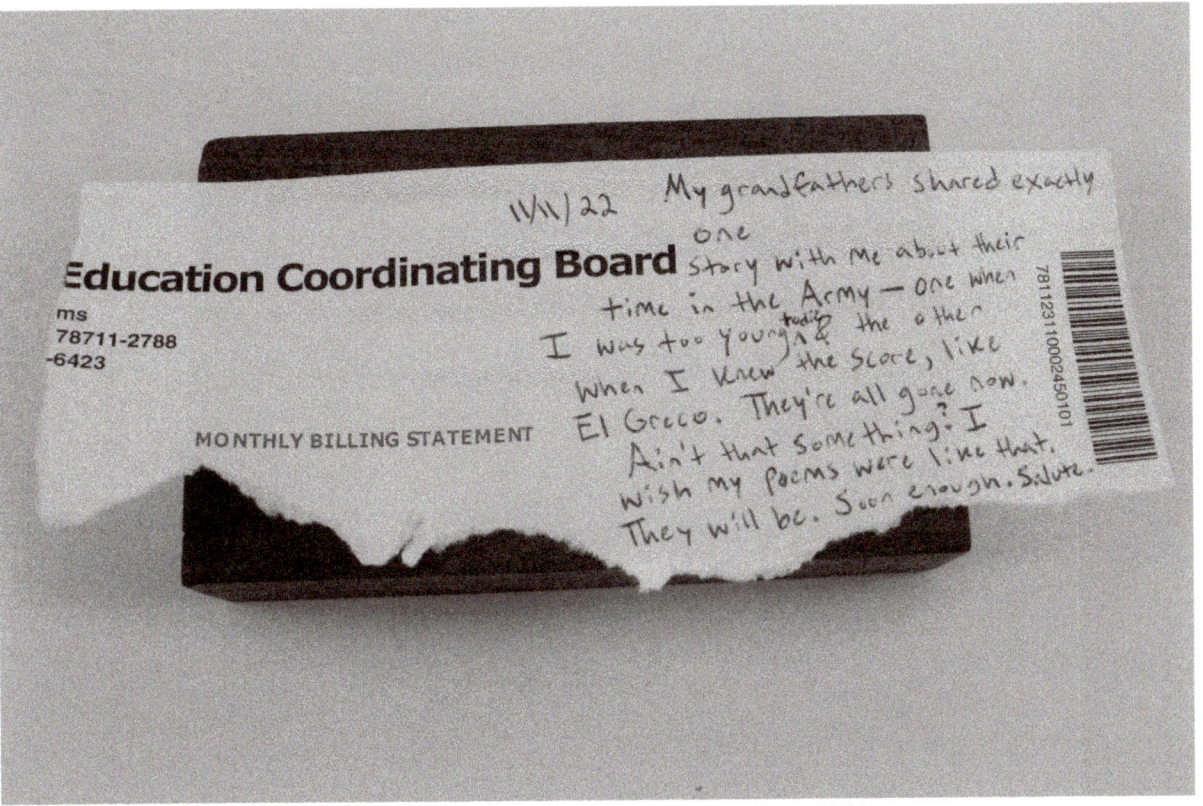

Man, I've dragged this BIC Atlantis places. The pen wouldn't leave me out of it, wasn't having it, today. I feel strangely called to forgive my legion of enemies imaginary & half real. But that's because I'm scared & my gaze is gravity-bent. Now I see Sylvia Plath on the wall & ~~can~~ can't imagine she'd be thrilled ~~about this~~. My friend, the poet Aaron Rudolph, is addicted to penning trash poems & sorry, brotha, but I'm ~~thrilled~~ ~~totes~~ thrilled. After 2 mighty swats a gnat replanted on my bicep — it just wants to ~~be~~ make friends. Half the time, the natural world is that way. Right? Lord, thank you for putting me back in. Letting me play the game my way.

White-napkin poem No. 23 (pg. 178)

Education Coordinating Board

ms
78711-2788
-6423

MONTHLY BILLING STATEMENT

11/11/22 My grandfathers shared exactly one story with me about their time in the Army — one when I was too young, today the other when I knew the score, like El Greco. They're all gone now. Ain't that something? I wish my poems were like that. They will be. Soon enough. Salute.

781123110002450101

Monthly billing statement poem (pg. 178)

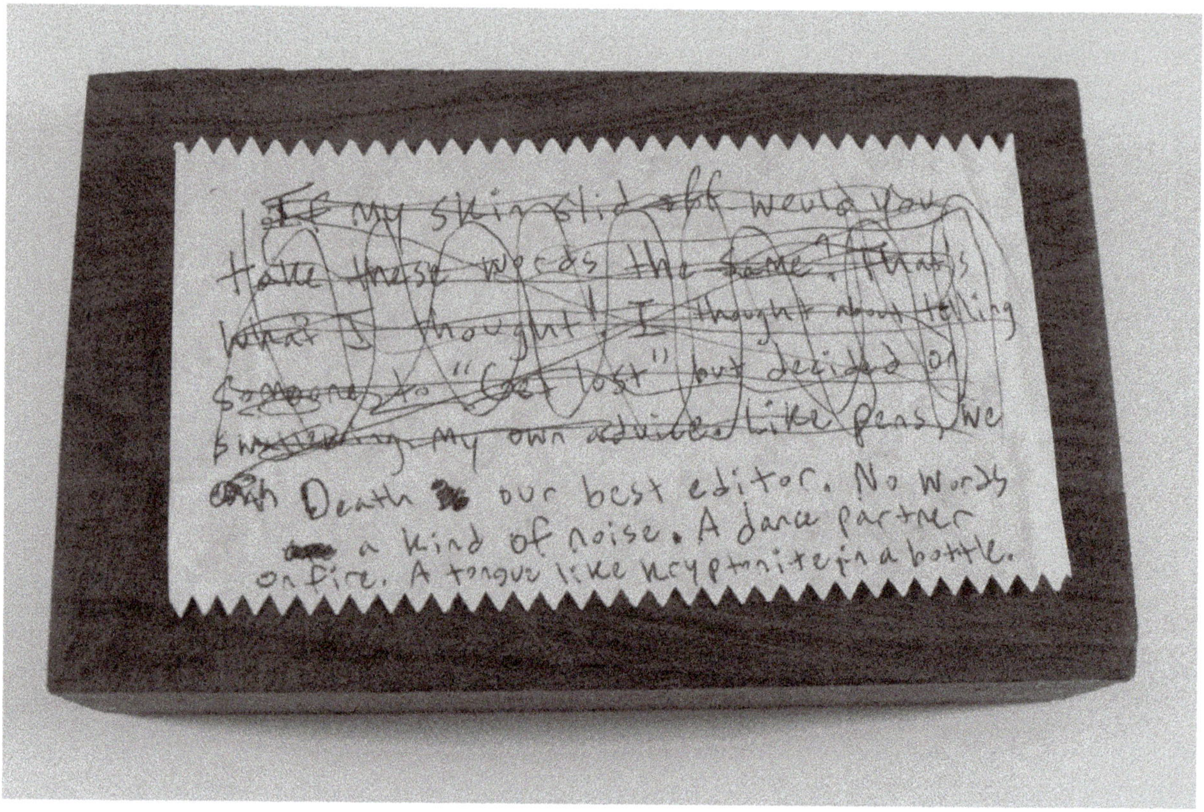

Gum-wrapper poem No. 38 (pg. 179)

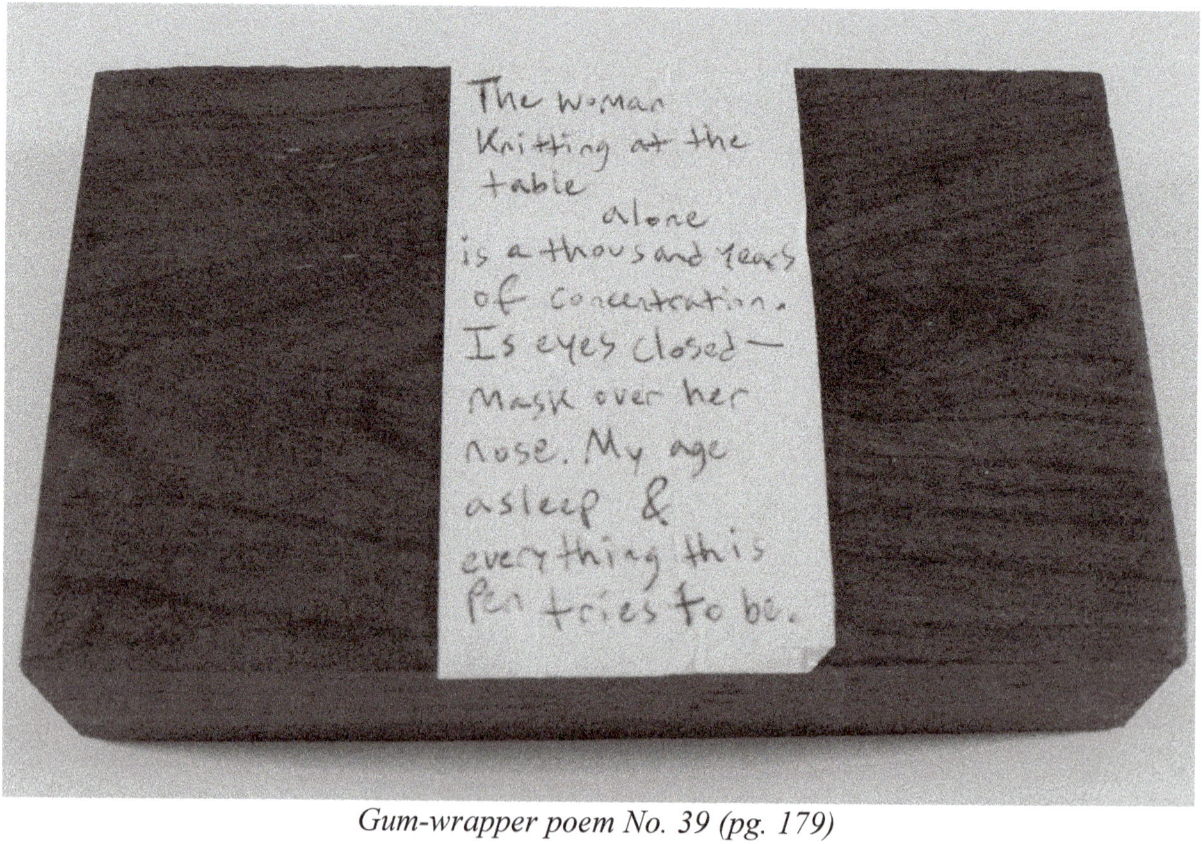

Gum-wrapper poem No. 39 (pg. 179)

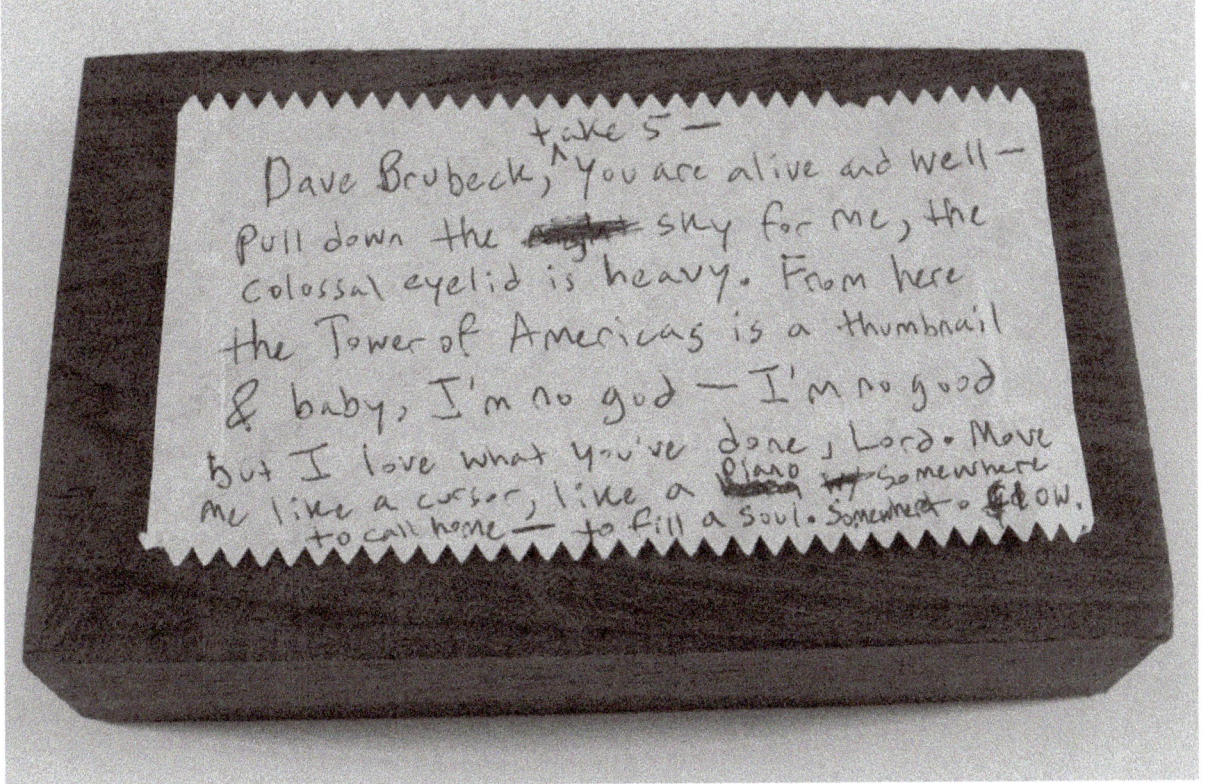

Notepad poem No. 5 (pg. 180)

Gum-wrapper poem No. 40 (pg. 180)

There's no such thing as a free poem.
Ha! I've ~~long~~ wanted to ~~get~~ that out.
Something has troubled me lately •
and it is this: my last ^grandma saw her pa
in my face, which she held in her frail
grip like a pail of holy water —
My hairline and white tips the
spitting image of a ~~paterfamilia~~ I never knew
but whose ~~shell~~ I've grown into ~~~~.
She did the sign of the cross and I
crossed my legs and tried to finish •
my barbecue in good faith. Do I
believe in ghosts? When I was just past
the point of sacrificing my soul to literature
and just before the point at smashing my •
head against a brick wall, I saw Roberto
Bolaño ^assuage ~~~~ me: "It's alright, fly under
my wings," and his leather jacket became
the ^permanent night and the ^silver pen my bleeding heart —
My sword, my flight — there is nothing I write
you can kill me with. Here, I'm already dead!
I mean this in good faith — there's no such
thing as a free life. Usher me from room to room
like a ~~true~~ host, break bread to Nat King Cole. Rest
my head on the bed of your breast. Thread — the
thin red thread.

Brown-bag poem (pg. 181)

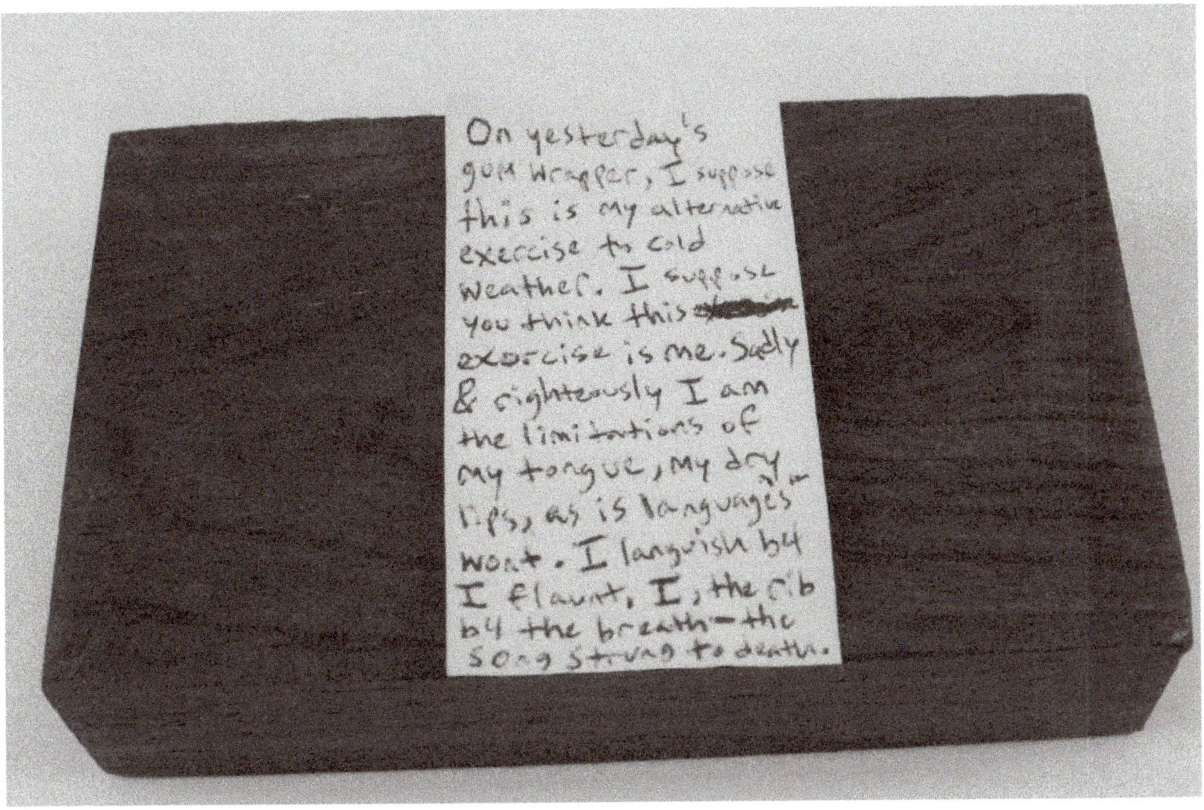

Gum-wrapper poem No. 41 (pg. 181)

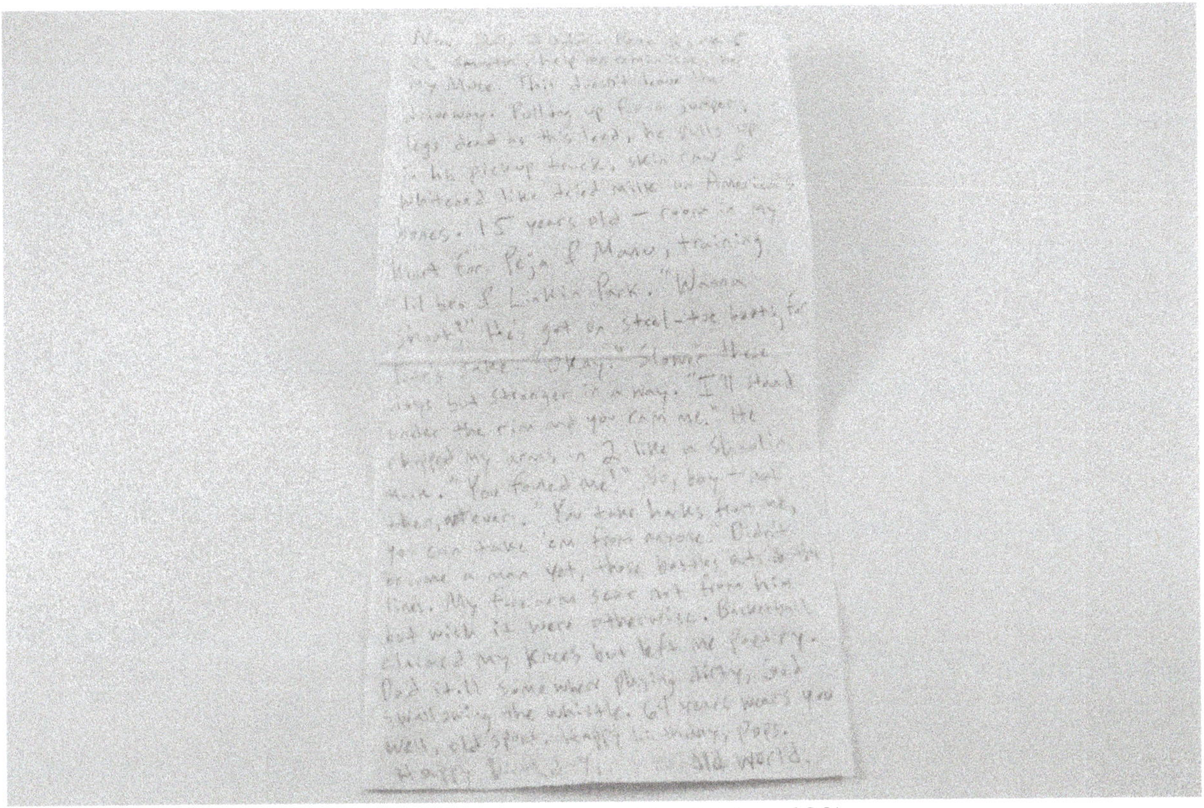

White-napkin poem No. 24 (pg. 182)

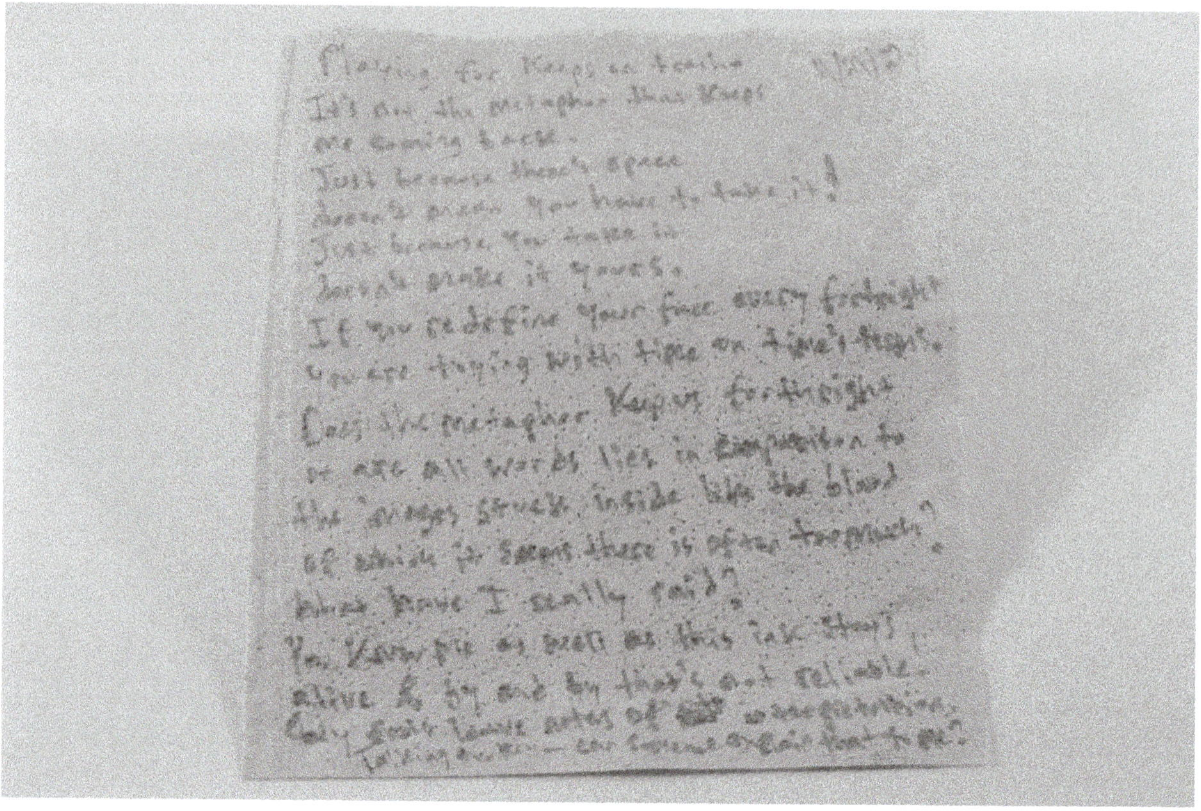

Brown-napkin poem No. 23 (pg. 183)

McDonald's coffee-cup poem No. 3 (pg. 184)

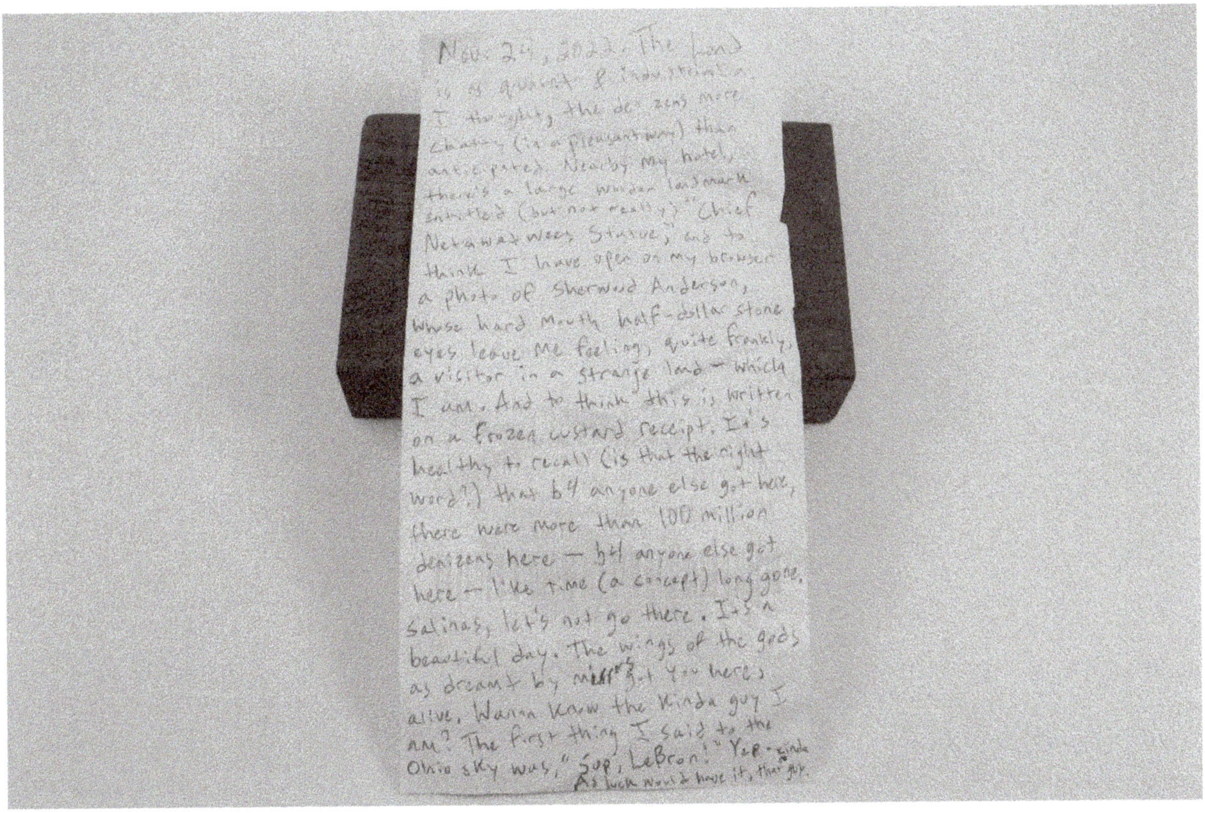

Receipt poem No. 3 (pg. 186)

Snack Mix poem (pg. 186)

Quivering quarters quartering quails.
Quails quartering quarters quivering.
Quarter-quails quivering quartering.
Quarter-quivering quails quartering.
Quarters quivering quail-quartering.

Quartering quivering quail quarters.

Quarter-quartering—quivering quails.

Quivering quail-quarters—quartering?

(You get the picture.)

P.S. I'm quivering kicking a cold. 11/27/22

White-napkin poem No. 25 (pg. 187)

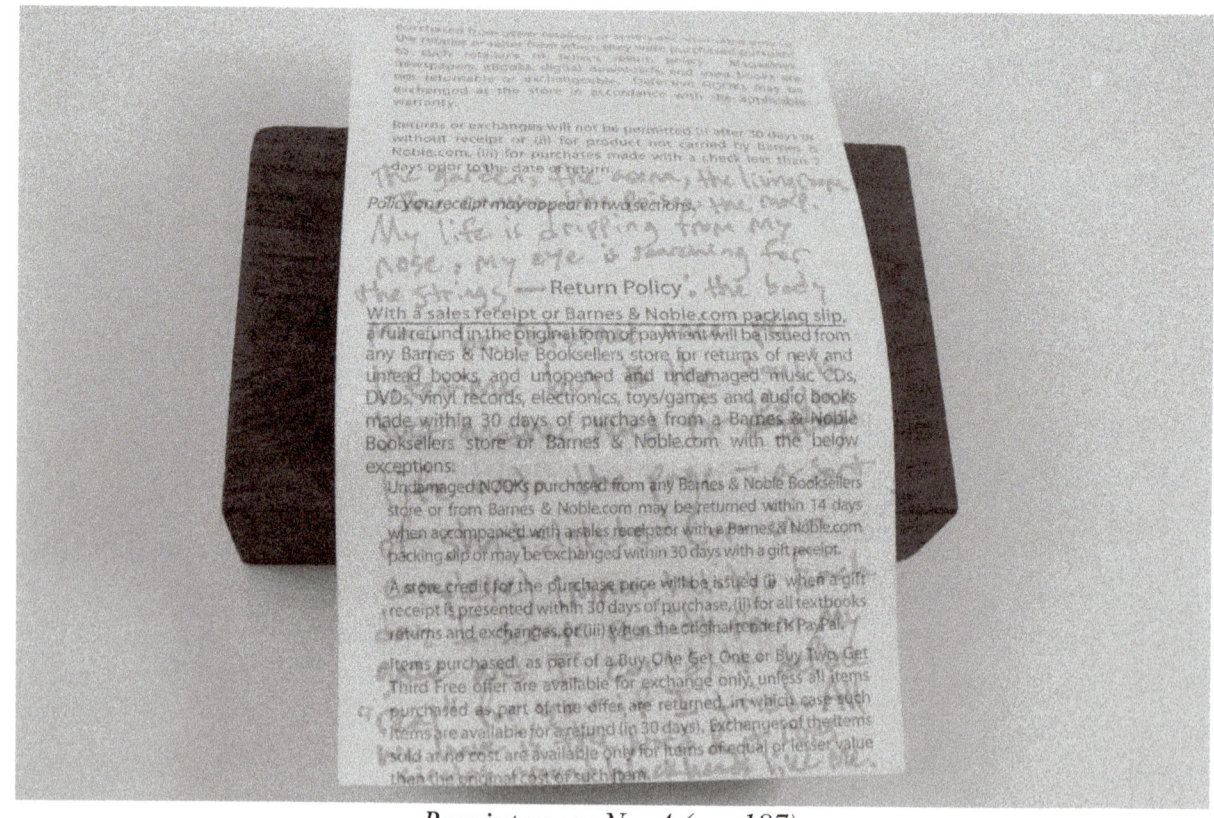

Receipt poem No. 4 (pg. 187)

It's funny — no smell
does have a kind of smell
but like my olfactory receptors
I opt to bypass its description.
Which has always been
the hoarsest aspect of my Pen.
You can call it work
insomuch that I'm likely
a bad boss to myself.
Or what some dub
a "players' coach."

There's no greater athlete than
Time —
each of us tugged
at the end of the line.
But I like to think of that
fabled runner as
kind enough to wait up for us,
rain or . . .
what some dub a soft touch.
It's true — you can't make a poem
w/o breaking a few eggs.
Grandpa hated eggs. He was not
a scribe, making my job easier
and unfathomably treacherous.
I've no desire to resurrect the dead
w/ the sorcery of select symbols —
a lie on select nights.
When the writer claimed the Word
saved her, I knew she was a
pufferfish. If the headless
bones of Shakespeare still expect
their audience, why shouldn't
there be those among us who delight
in the indoctrination of poison?

Receipt poem No. 5 (pg. 188)

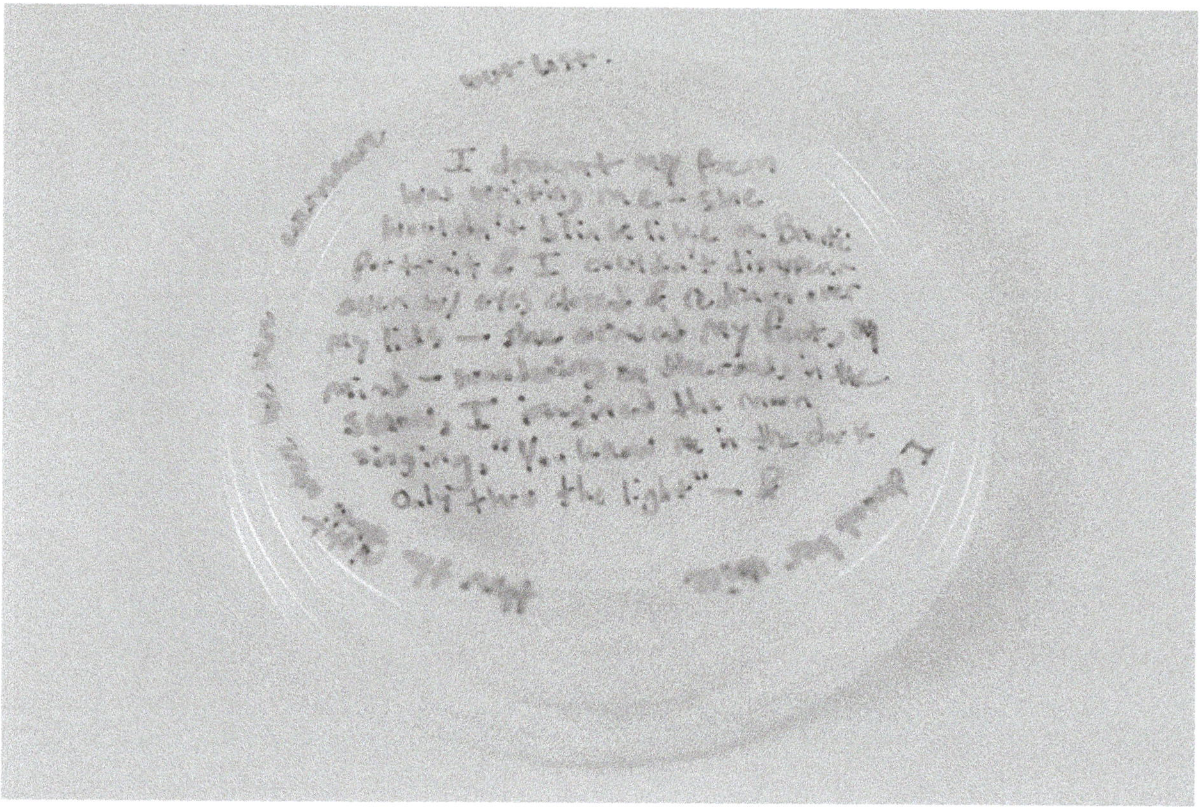

Water-lid poem No. 2 (pg. 189)

Gum-wrapper poem No. 42 (pg. 189)

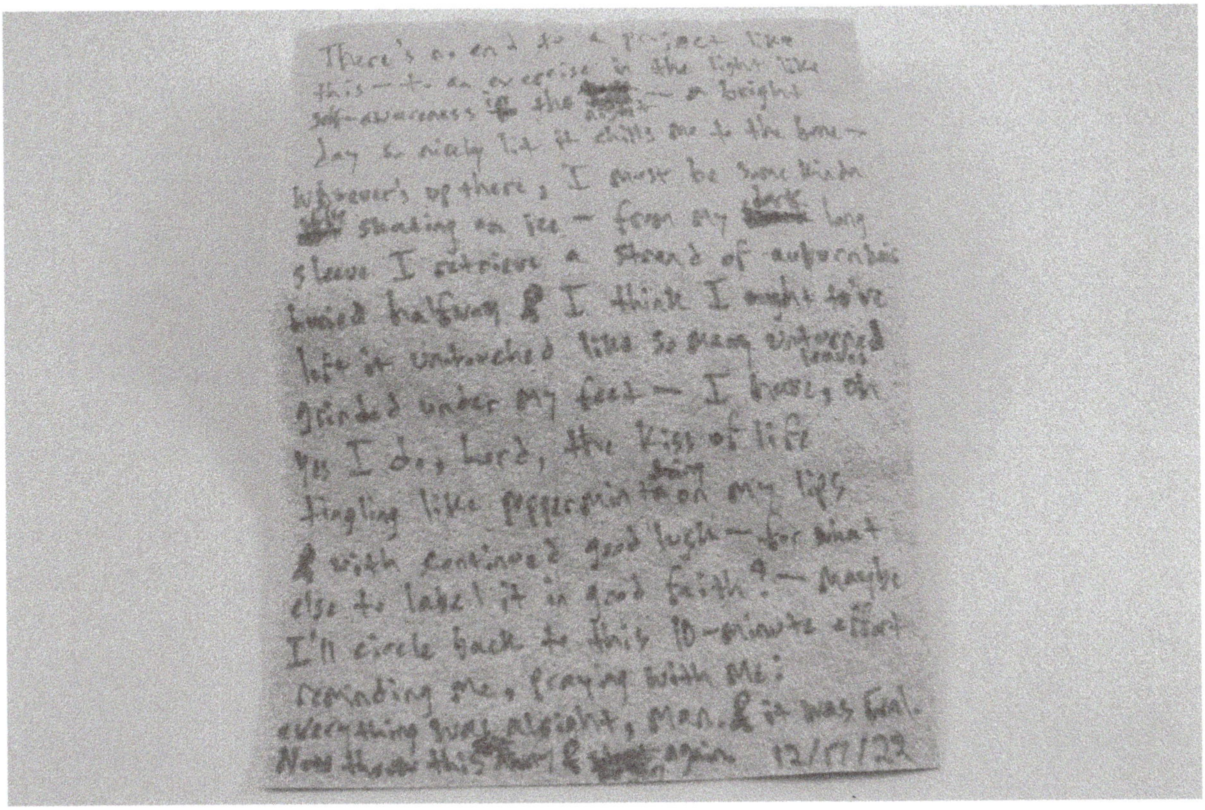

Brown-napkin poem No. 24 (pg. 190)

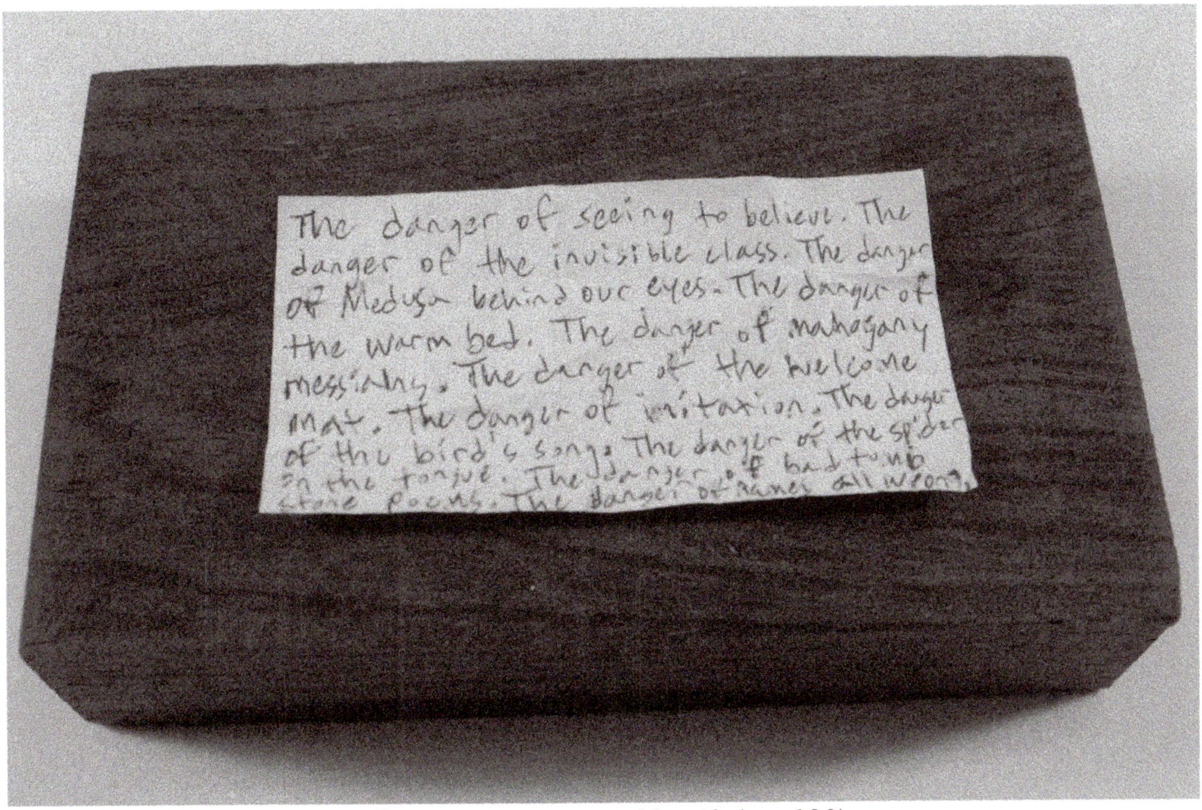

Gum-wrapper poem No. 43 (pg. 190)

I wanted to sit at the very edge of my
chair & report like a clairvoyant
the true skeleton voided by the horizon
but the biting haze of my coffee gives
way to a ~~intuition~~ ~~berth~~ — that I
glow only in your embrace on the scant
mornings ~~after~~ we share like two chess pieces
holding the line long after the last battle
cry has evaporated in the ~~threat~~ maw of some
opaque maker or other — wasn't it just
dusk, lover? Wasn't the grime of young
Patti Smith's vinyled vocals the shot of life
most divine, as if the sky brightened in your
eyes? ~~was it~~ Pushed to the edge again — sunk & ~~told~~ blind.

White-napkin poem No. 26 (pg. 191)

35 degrees. Somewhere in the American Southwest it
seemed to the poet, writing on a napkin, that our lives —
the lived ones, the ones cut short — amounted to
one unanswerable question. (More than fair, the
frigid air.) He sat fleshing from limb to soul
a character who'd wield an antique sword
in her own backyard when a man in a
North Face jacket w/ coffee in hand approached
him & inquired about the spilled contents of his
pen. Also: the books by his side (by Wanda Coleman
& Denis Johnson). "You get paid for your work?"
asked he, to which the other replied, "You
offering me an honorarium?" The man said,
"Nice shoes — have a ~~kickin'~~ day," & like that
there was hardly room for anything else — not his
10-year-old Air Force Ones, not the stable stage of a
table setting this poem, not the kiss of life on his lips,
not the cashless wallet resting by his hip. A lifetime
of religion hadn't prepared him for this — not quite, not
~~precisely~~. For who will undo all the bad words? (This question
shouldn't concern the ~~real~~ poet.) In due time, the slate
will be swiped clean — the napkin will whimper in the
dustbin of history, & she who wielded the sword will
take w/ her to the grave a mystery unknowable to even
~~she~~ — all outside my own backyard! In my own
lifetime. How the trees in the city are like small
green explosions & they are in this together! (Mostly?)
How they grow for us in this besainted & quartered
body politic so-called safe from the trappings of darkness
by Adam's kind. The long line spread thin like a malnourished
platoon lost in the roots of some untranslated master-plan.
to follow the sunset & hope for peace in a mad dash for

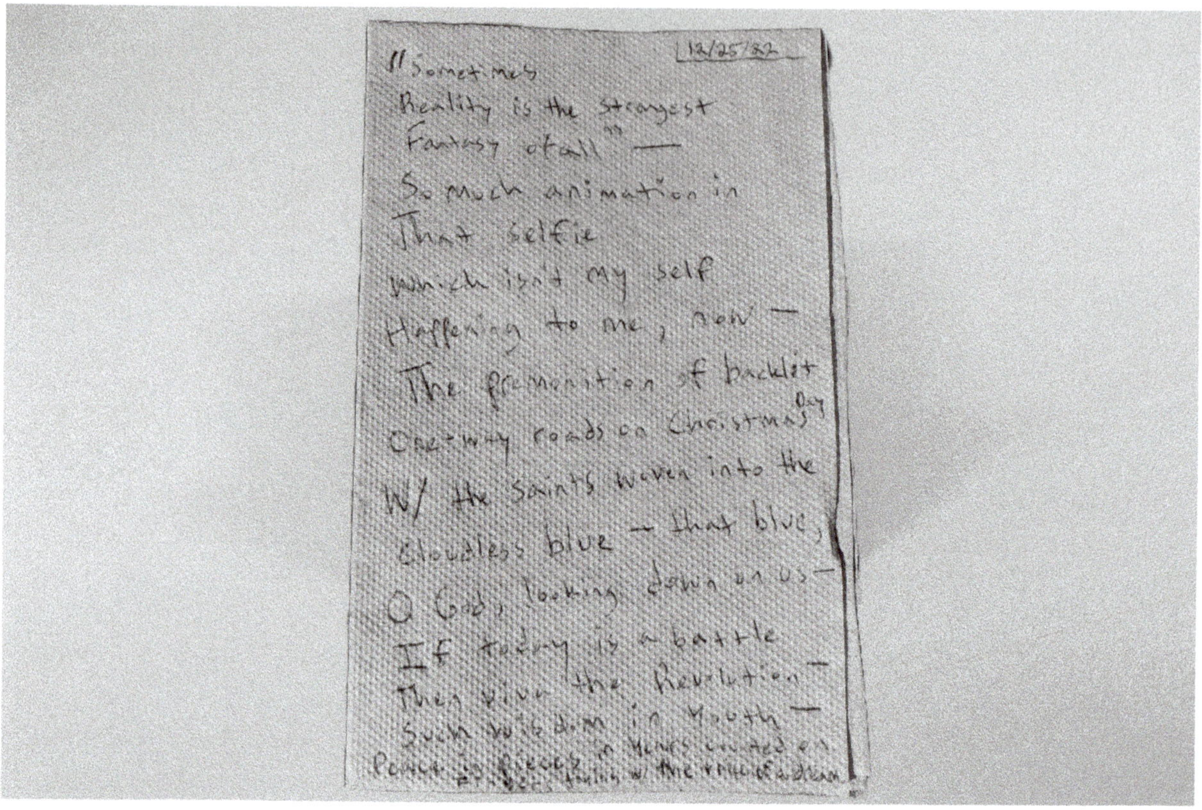

Brown-napkin poem No. 26 (pg. 193)

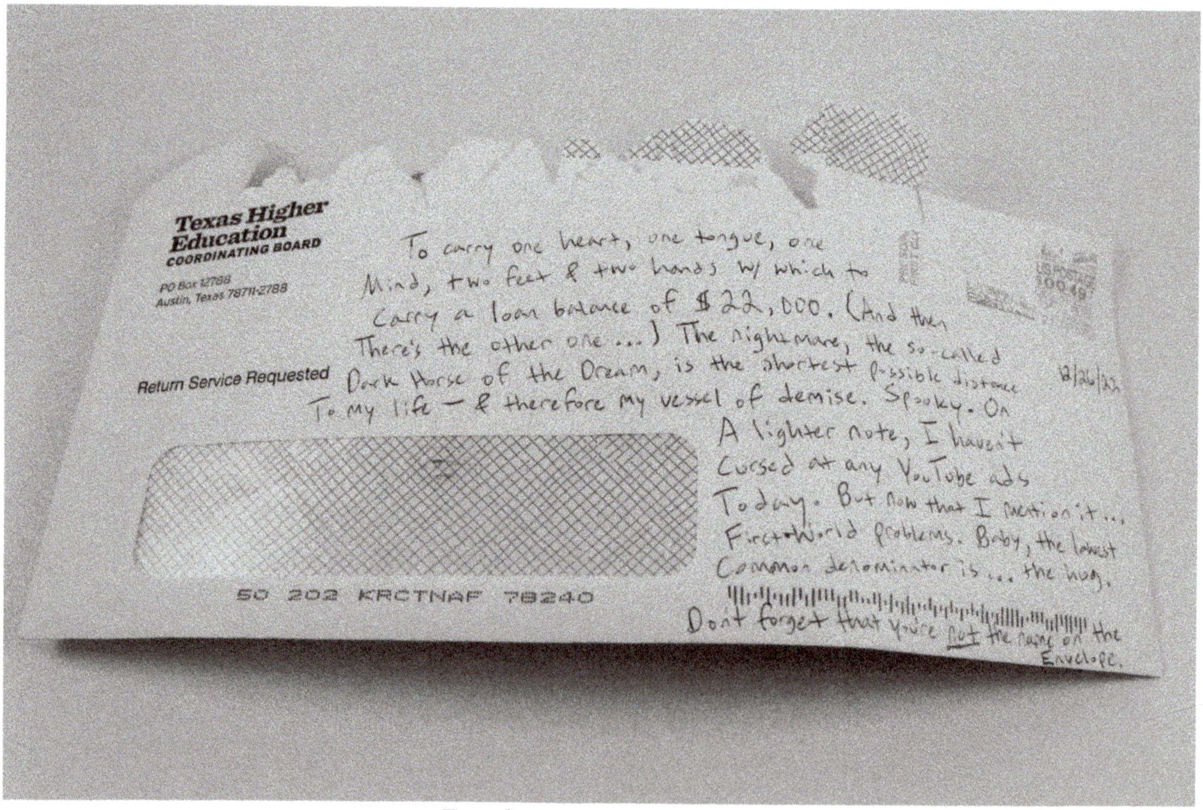

Envelope poem (pg. 193)

Leaf poem (pg. 194)

Korean pagoda & red oaks, turtles lining the pond's edge w/ sun-craned necks like cypress stumps, Aldo Leopold's prose in our ears — thus began our new year, Love — the treaded trail of conservation labyrinthine — 67 degrees, post-freeze, SATx. Napkins & coffee sleeves have suffered mightily on my watch. (All trash poetry is trash talk.) Stop — whosoever said to end not w/ a bang but a whimper — agreed — but we're basically idiots. 4-5 books at any given time in my knapsack. At any given time, my spine be like: "Seriously, jackass?" Half the time the answer's always "yes." Many moons ago my moon was already Christ's moon & Senator Pilate's moon. In

other words, my moon was my mother's, first. & yours first, too. To think the africanized bee almost stung you. There one. The bloated world less than a period among many stars from afar. & w/o you: almost nothing any more. Or something else entirely. & I realize: writing to you is like never dying. Writing is bleeding & never dying. That's why I carry more reading than I can chew. That's why I take this gift & give it back to you. God help me. Trapped & freed. 1/1/23

Gift-card sleeves poem (pg. 195)

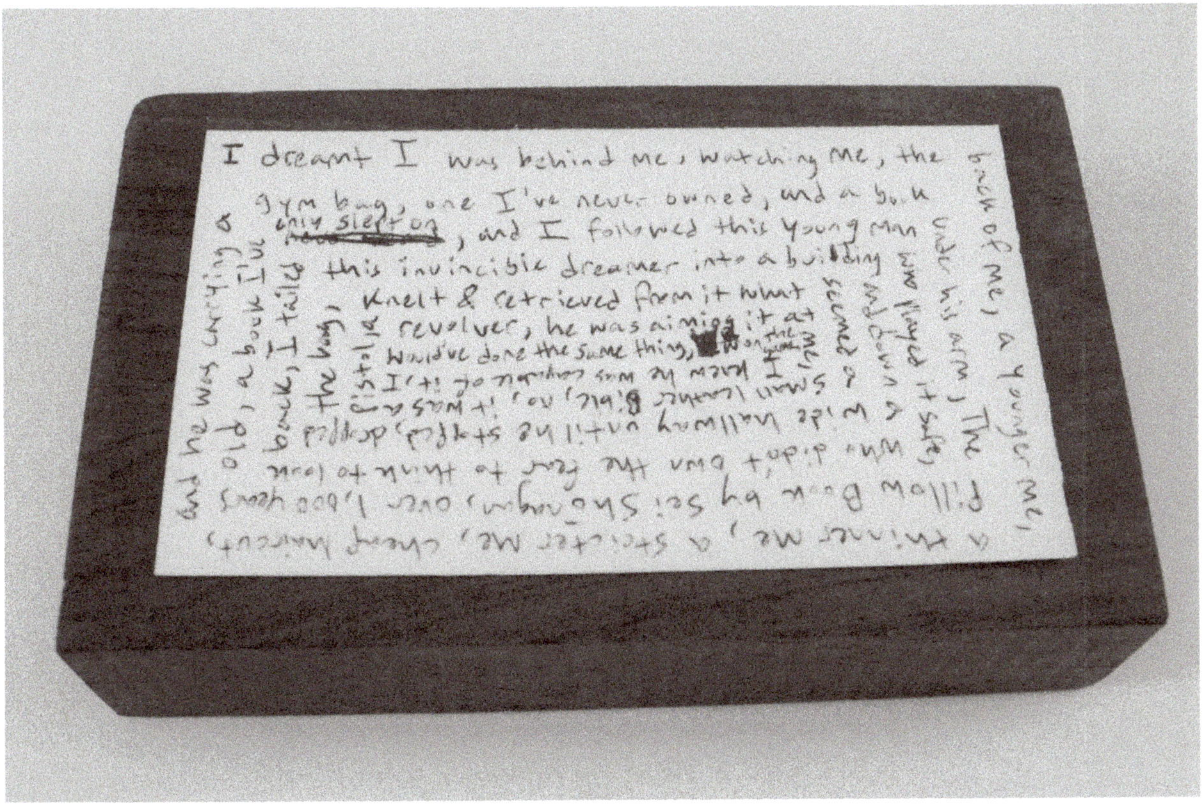

Business-card poem (pg. 196)

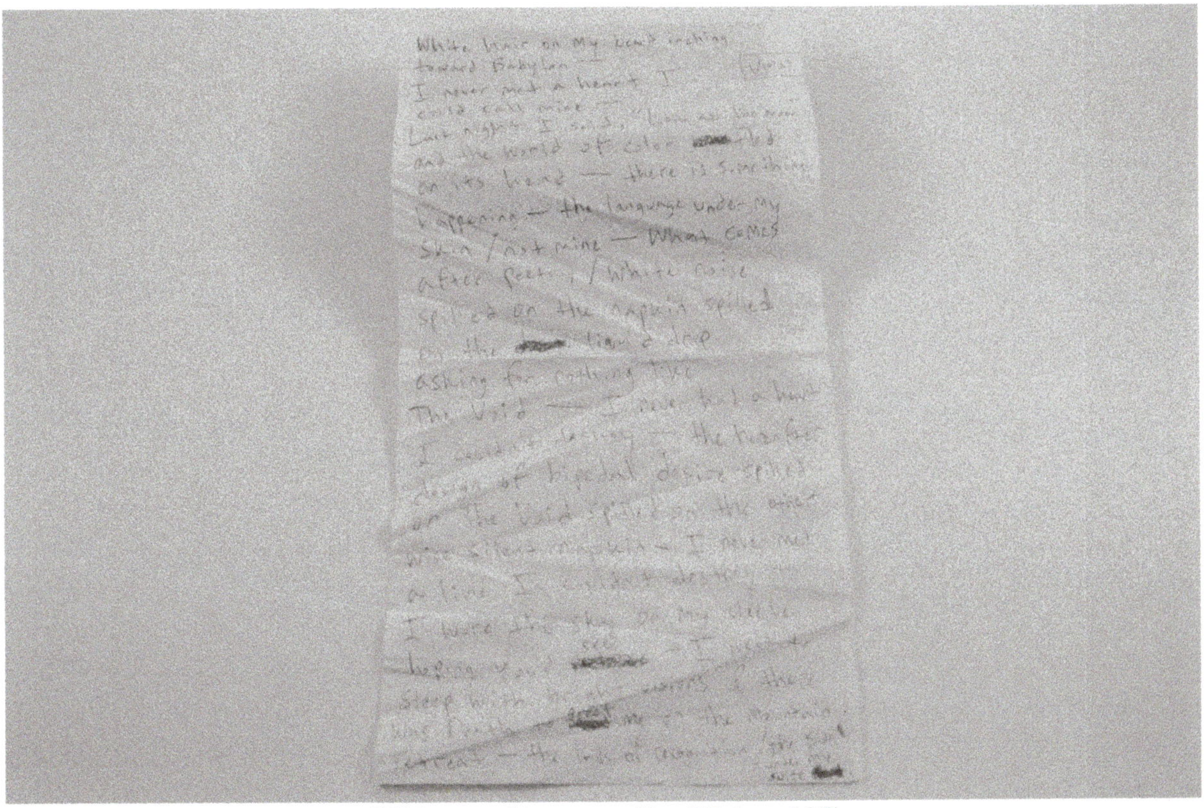

White-napkin poem No. 27 (pg. 197)

Up 1604 & the panzers of intelligence
Around me the whipping speed
Why nobody's come at me with
"Harmony's nickname can only be
Harm"
Is because they're wise not to lend literature
Lines the foolish streetwise panthers of
Intelligence surrounding everywhere the
Whipping harmony of mornings splashed down
Caromed chrome crossings God why has
Nobody told me how it'd be
Is that a gasoline tank or lunchbox in her
Hands is she still loved from the ground up
Well hell — she's crying laughing. 1/12/23

White-napkin poem No. 28 (pg. 198)

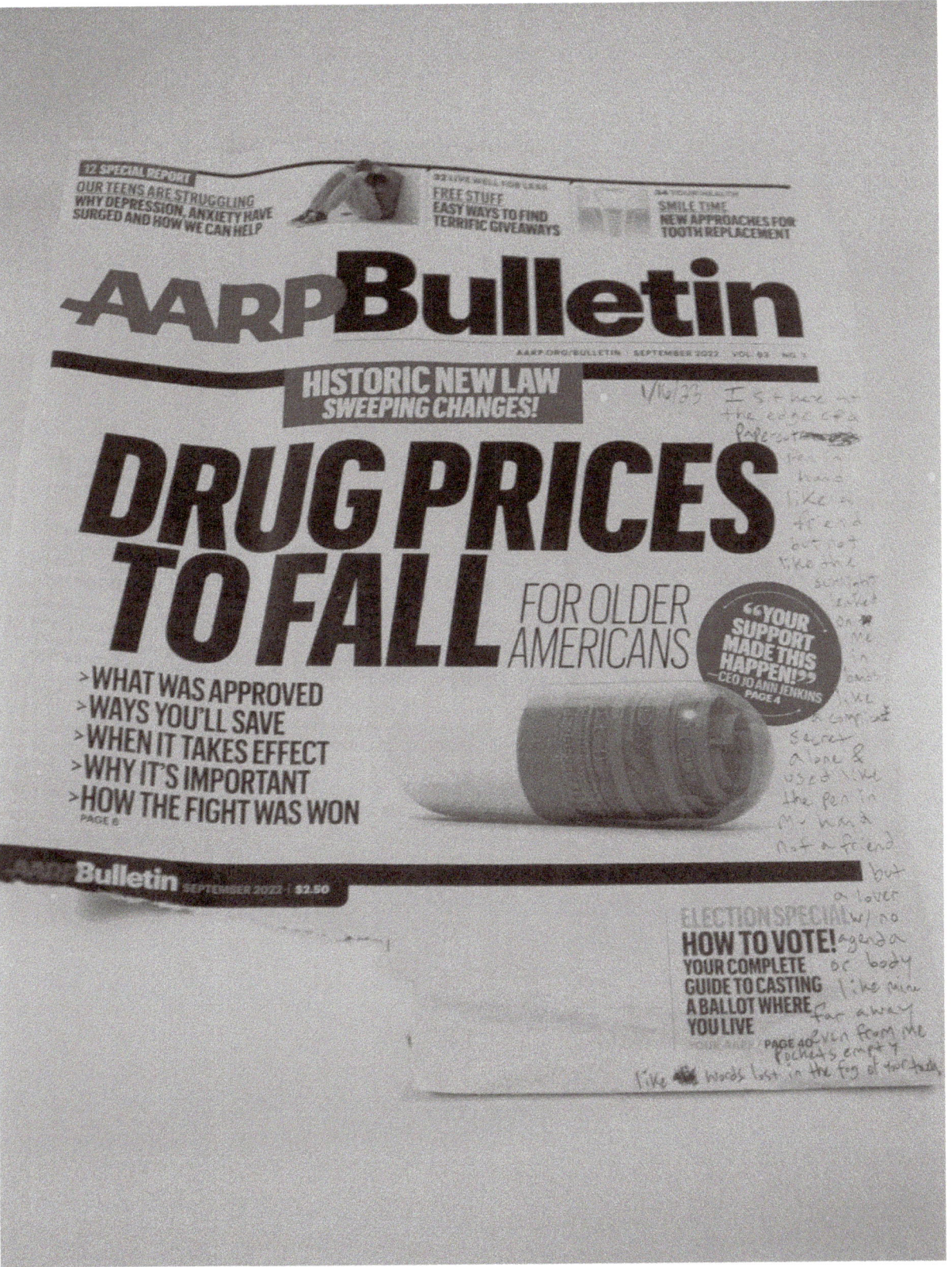

AARP Bulletin poem (pg. 199)

Chopstick poem (pg. 200)

Gum-wrapper poem No. 44 (pg. 200)

Plastic-knife poem (pg. 201)

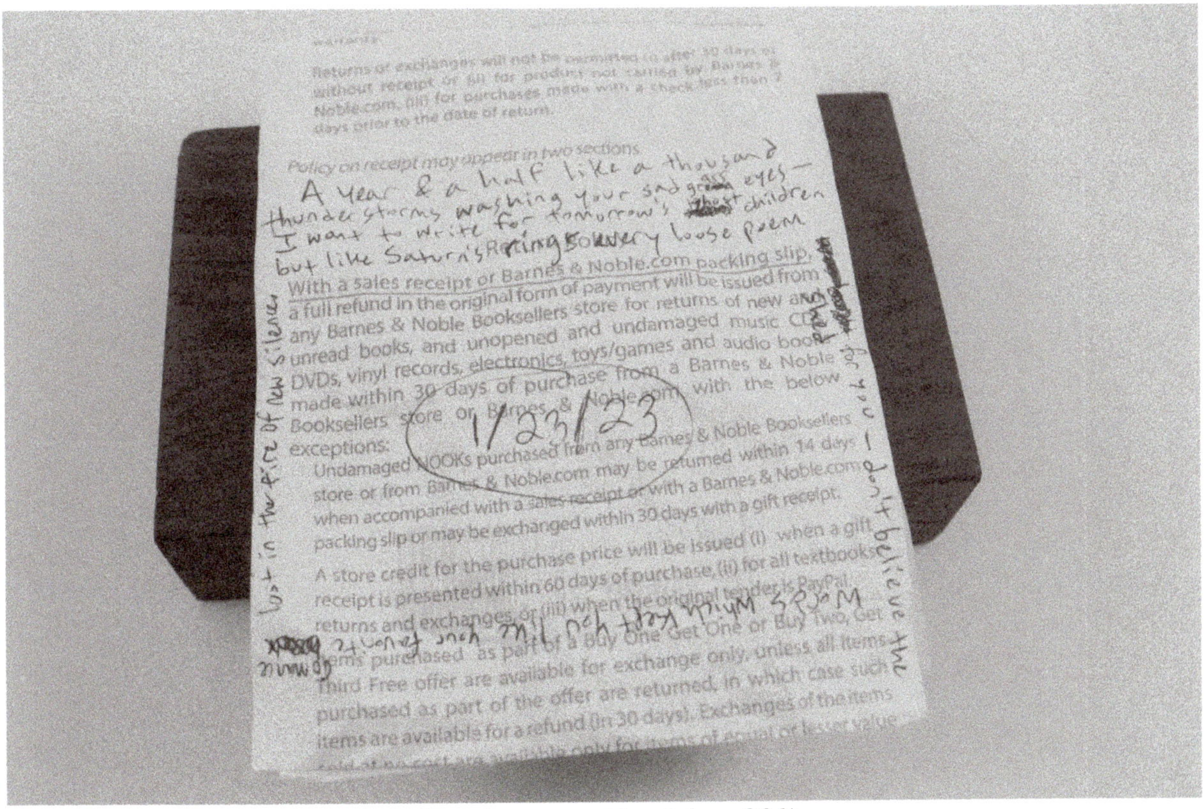

Receipt poem No. 6 (pg. 201)

Gum-wrapper poem

Present passed
Measured delay
Theoreticals & smelly
Spray
#1 cause of perfume:
Death
Spearmint breath / car plumes
Extra gum never hurt anyone!

Gum-wrapper poem No. 2

Cicada shell baking on
Adobe wall
Specter of
Marx's beard
Spread wide on
Mien of
Liver jam / Smucker's brand
Oh man!
Cosmopolitan foil-wrap oblivion.

6/24/21

Gum-wrapper poem No. 3

Saw a dude w/ pants
Halfway down
Red briefs
Thought, Every punk who's
Screwed me over has worn
An expensive belt.

Gum-wrapper poem No. 4

It's Friday in Austin &
The Nike store employee
Gently discards my book
Recommendation while in my
Hands Enrique Vila-Matas
Propagates "literature sickness"—
No cure, I inform my satellite heart.

Red-napkin poem

Occurred to me suddenly
I'm less Jesus cuz I don't
Drink /
On my blacklist similarly:
Sweet Texas iced tea /
Lack & slack, sloppy relief /
Brief prayer, red napkin reprieve:
God, Mama Mary—
Pearly Pete,
Will you grant my entry
Pretty please?

6/26/21

Coffee-sleeve poem

Kiss goodbye
Emerald eyes
Morning light
Inside my
Steel
Lozenge
Plunging
Down
Earth's
Windpipe.

Gum-wrapper poem No. 5

Why can't the good live
Forever?
Sister who learned my name
Gene Wilder's voice
Alley where we bargained w/
God / filled with brick
Dead bumblebee in a crack of
Concrete—
Lotus at my front door.

6/28/21

Coffee-sleeve poem No. 2

8:04 a.m. and the SA sky is
Halfway between letting us have it
And Seattle freeze /
"Come and take it," I dare the
Saints above the Alamo in my
Heart's eye /
Weather like this makes me wanna
Hide inside black coffee, this
Starbucks sleeve / peel it back
But I might bleed.

Coffee-sleeve poem No. 3

Rain falls /
Poetry grinds
the
Beautiful & lost /
What you cannot say, write /
What you cannot write,
Curse the clouds.

Flip-book poem

I
dreamt
a
teal
cyclops
Told
me
about
the
reconstruction
of
Jericho
where
Shakespeare
is
Queen
and
~~poets~~ archaeologists
are
police.

Letterhead poem

My shirt reads:
"Freedom is never free"
And it's true if you
Pry my chest open
Find my mind a time-
Hardened center
Choosing brutal
Poetry against
The Void—
Goodbye, University of
The Underground—
Dangerous discourse
Always felt safe.

7/01/21

Gum-wrapper poem No. 6

Bukowski's *Factotum* joined me at
The gym. Nobody asked about it.
Would've claimed research for work
Which is true / but what's real? Are
You real? Am I? Who since '17 has
Stood substantial? My front tires low
I stall as tho today's rain floods me
W/ purpose, which is factual—I think fast
W/ a damp crown—
Verses drown.

Gum-wrapper poem No. 7

I accept John Cheever as my
Master today—"The Enormous Radio"
Prelude to privacy's invasion via
Fingertips / something alien, pokey,
Hokey / hocus pokey lickety-split
Today, JC, you are my Father—
This poem I offer as gift & sacrifice
(Behind bowed back, my fingers crossed).

Gum-wrapper poem No. 8

Like Alejandro Zambra
The only thing literature
Taught me is
I like to read /
When it pours, poke holes in
American cinema /
No, no tears here—
It's only rain.

Coffee-sleeve poem No. 4

This
pigeon
bopping
its
head
to
Childish
Gambino / Beyond
my vision a
poem
swaying
w/o
shame /
Sketch
the action
from
behind,
my
flesh
fades.

Gum-wrapper poem No. 9

I'm an all-around
MF-er, said my
friend in the USA—
John Dos Passos'
chosen country where
southern sun's ruthless
rays invade northbound,
heat bubbles inside which
proper words melt off my
tongue—malt-style—
stain crumpled pages
contained within the
cocoon of my home in the
chosen country of
ghosts I cross through
every morning outside
my front door.

7/11/21

Gum-wrapper poem No. 10

Literature is hell /
Heaven is hell /
Heaven is South Texas /
S. TX is hell /
Remember the Alamo /
Remember time did not
save Proust—
Proust did not save
time—not even
Proust / I bid thee
adieu on trash /
Time is trash, poetry is
trash / Pray at the
altar of Trash /
O beautiful shroud.

7/12/21

Gum-wrapper poem No. 11

I see you, Vincent Cooper of
Zarzamora Street whose face like
Mine doesn't suit your name—
Whose relatives like mine were beaten
Into bone by bullets & booze /
Our dead—eternal masters /
The living rooms seemed
So much
larger.

Brown-napkin poem

I want to touch those
Clouds at the end of my
Sight
I want to fill this scroll
(not a napkin, a scroll)
To its very end like Kerouac
I want to turn my cold coffee into
Iced water
And to turn my back and
Find my long-lost friend
Who chose to lose himself in
The city—
Or something like my dreams.

Coffee-sleeve poem No. 5

Most things break
Down
Within 3 questions /
We're left to
Tango w/ Dr. Seuss
And other cute-sounding
Noise /
I once told someone
Verbatim: "A
Gentle nudge is lesser
Than a poke & mightier
Than an elbow" /
I once told somebody:
"Sort out the white space
For your own good" /
Then I snapped awake
From daydream and
Poetry wrecked me
Again / It's punitive
This thing like chewing
Time like a sweet stick
Of gum /
My breath still stinks
And the seconds scream
Like a grandfather
Clock on fire.

7/17/21

White-napkin poem

Baby, I'm no Neruda but
Have you ever been asked upon a
Dying man's gasping last breath
Are you happy?
I relive this everyday and you
Your hair the color of my blood /
This, the sweetest thing I'm capable of
Writing today
Dancing to Sharon Jones w/ hand
Choking the pen
Launching choice words for bad verse to
My heart—south of heart—
Land of Conrad's madness &
Ticking stars—your eyes among them in
My night sky.

Brown-napkin poem No. 2

It's entirely possible to
Discover after a snowstorm a
Voice like the dragonfly I
Noticed this morning entombed
Behind mesh wire—pardon
Brother, I darken amid daylight
But it'd be you to see beauty in
Mummies—bug mummies—
Eyes of the living past like a
Godhead, dried shells, those
New Mexico mountains across
From which you dwelled & call home
Or close to it or far & wide like the
Sombrero Galaxy where your poems
Are headed at the speed of light.

7/19/21

Gum-wrapper poem No. 12

The dead hold
Our interest like
Elvis clings to
Myth—mystic
Sideburns /
From deep under-
Ground music
Seems close to
Mute &
Yesterday's
Kings are
Rock.

7/20/21

Coffee-sleeve poem No. 6

My father once said
White people rule countries better
And I never responded
No, killing legally—
Because I love my father
And he loves me
And there
Was always
A vague
Unspecificity
About
Our
Conve-
Rsations
And my pale, beautiful brothers &
Sisters see me when I'm there—
I don't always want to be there
Because love only
Stretches so
Thin.

Gum-wrapper poem No. 13

Don't have it
Today—
Emptied the pack
And nothing special in
That—
Save your imagery—
My "I" in dreams—
Mother sol, our
Circular nature—
Empire undone
By will of
Fire.

7/22/21

Coffee-cup poem

Come to Wong's &
Chill / bring a bud
Talk race politics &
Appetite of the city
Crawling toward
Change—all good
Nature of reality
God in the air—
OK, my friend's
Calling / chicken &
Waffles /
Fahrenheit 209
I'll be back.

Gum-wrapper poem No. 14

Ideas so big,
Script so fine /
Mechanism thru which to say
I love you /
Dusk so deep & blue
How many kisses
Goodbye
Left in my
Tank?

7/28/21

Gum-wrapper poem No. 15

Those who bemoan
Restless minds
Will be dust a
Long long time—
Live long in this
Silly compression
On this piece of trash
Held intact by laws
Beyond my grasp &
Adored by far 2 few—
To breathe & move is
Reason for
Celebration!

7/30/21

Gum-wrapper poem No. 16

I read to inspire my
Writing, write to inspire
My living—jumble the
Verbs around, makes zero
Difference to me—
I've studied crucifixes
So long I pity the
Bloodied lamb & find in
Song pathways of cathedral
Ceilings I've dreamt of
Crawling upon—our collective
Flesh should house only
One tattoo
(Font of your choosing):
You've No Earthly Clue

8/01/21

Brown-napkin poem No. 3

If you seek Beauty
You are a narcissist
Which is to say
A child of God
But so as to not isolate my
Nonbelieving friends
I jot these thoughts on
Trash past its functionality to
Prove or suggest the
Power of Beauty at its
Darkest—how I shunned my
Principles & safety to see myself
In a blood-toned woman because
You
Told me
You loved me
The first
Time we
Kissed
Because color is love so potent
It begs like fruit to be
Sucked dry
Or worship only the ground.

Gum-wrapper poem No. 17

If like a sunbaked
Detective or a
Bloodhound I traced
The scent of my roots
Would invisible trail
Lines map the face of
God? Not the best
Question, untrained
In artistry & police
Work—I read a
Backwards poem thru
A mirror & the space
Between time called
Crying & said:
When you coming
Home?

8/05/21

Gum-wrapper poem No. 18

Stephen King at it
Again & I on my
Archipelago of trash—
SOS—send bags of
Oreos, the pages of
Fran Ross—gift me
Anything & I'll stain it
W/ ink—seize my ink
And I think: I'm
Cooked, Tom Hanks,
Perfect storm—being
Man means any-
Thing may be my
Wilson.

8/06/21

Gum-wrapper poem No. 19

Pi is unsolvable &
Life's the perfect
Length by all measures—
Of course I don't
Mean humans—
I rip my fingernails &
Repurpose them as
Toothpicks—limited
Resources & eons
Plenty to waste all—
Fellow countrymen:
We are spectacular in
Estranging foreign dirt
Thru desert words.

8/08/21

Gum-wrapper poem No. 20

When Big Pun says
I'm not a player
I just crush a lot /
Death dipping her
Toesies in the pool /
Pocket full of
Trash / mad ankle
Rash—immortality
Allergies—the Void
Blows another kiss as
I spill irresponsibly &
Rather intentionally /
This poem master key
To cracking itself /
How bout this
Body?

8/10/21

Gum-wrapper poem No. 21

When Hegel says
Too fair to worship
Too divine to love /
When Jesus says
Love your enemies
The sun rises on evil too /
When the sun says
Chase me &
Mourn the night /
When the moon says
I lift oceans to
Get a rise out of you.

8/11/21

McDonald's coffee-cup poem

When Nate Dogg says
I'm listenin to a sad girl
Sing how she got her heart
Broke / if there's such
A thing as unpacking
I'm perpetually on the
Move / I write to redeem my-
Self—but from poetry's
Point of view? / feels like
Every great supper is the
Last / time is words &
Bodies are vanishing /
Rearranging / received a
Call just now from "Scam
Likely"—this, I know, to be
Undoubtedly true.

Brown-napkin poem No. 4

I told a friend recently I'm
Ashamed Ted Cruz owns a Spanish
Surname—and I'm ashamed for using
"Owns" and ashamed this is my 3rd
Poem featuring Cruz—but not ashamed
This is a trash poem, a spontaneous
Brown-napkin poem. A senator named
Cruz fled when ice settled in & folks
Froze to death in Texas. He could've
Been anyone but he is a
Cruz and I'm ashamed. How easily these
Words can be ash. How easily one can
Flee from a family poodle. Where is the
Honor, where is the love? Where's
Cruise control?

8/15/21

Brown-napkin poem No. 5

I am thankful I cannot see
At once
All (to quote Donald Barthelme)
The interacting tendencies of
This world /
I am thankful for space /
Mine no different from yours /
I am thankful for governance—I,
Spawn of white-knuckled lust /
Pawn, soldier up / knuckles broad &
Bony like Papa's—salute /
I stretched so thin / heart skin of
A water balloon /
I am thankful for slow daze at the
Office, the vacant kiss of a
Butterfly /
O Tunnel Vision, gorgeous goon—
You give me room to bleed &
Write.

Gum-wrapper poem No. 22

I am 1 day into a fresh fade & a few days
Away from a new book release—I am fading
Reasonably well to quote a reliably quotable old
Geezer—but tomorrow may change things & so
Allow me on trash to express today's being a good
Day as are most revolutions in this blissfully
Immature country—a lasagna of scrap & bones—
Nothing to josh about—O carpet, I must
Vacuum you for I am slowly becoming my
Mother—no Norman Bates.

Coffee-cup poem No. 3

Poetry—poster rat

Gum-wrapper poem No. 23

There's a difference between
Different and differing
Not
Dog & God /
I mean slush-eyed mop-drooped
Sopping love / me in meekness
We between
Weary and weakness.

9/03/21

Gum-wrapper poem No. 24

Salinas at it again w/ Trash Poems
W/ O'Hara's *Lunch Poems* on the
Dome—Norm Mickey D no more &
The weekend updates itself—
Gray eye of the sky stirs cruelty
In me—breeze so lovely but
Who'll fuck it up?

Gum-wrapper poem No. 25

Something familiar &
Uncomfortable about
Edward Norton's vibe,
Incongruous ensemble of
Features on a great
American face, our
Names & voices, land of
Wailing mothers, blue
So sparingly found in
Nature except the eyes
Of our favored sons—
Ask Toni Morrison,
God rest her words—
It's a majestic day in
America, inner weather
Permitting.

Brown-napkin poem No. 6

Something about a loud voice in a cafe—
Follow me across the city
Across the collision of appetites—
Something about the space never felt right—
According to the pen all palms are tender
To the touch—
There aren't enough napkins for you—
The covering of mouths under gray clouds
Leaves eyes open to invasion—
Love as one prolonged sexy goodbye—
Here I trap the hopscotch of a man
In a parking lot
Who seems to embrace the familiar horror of
Rush hour as the cool air mummifies my throat
Making an instant snack outta my chewing gum
As I repeat these words aloud
Finding concealed stories in every crack
Between the teeth of the earth
And did I mention
There aren't enough napkins?
The madman across a 4-way
Crucifying it w/ jazz fingers &
The nails of invisible notes.

Brown-napkin poem No. 7

She took her chocolate pie recipe
With her to the grave
And the sweetness drifts
Beyond my tongue
As the black shirts in my closet
Swallow every "thank you"
I failed to give.

11/20/21

Brown-napkin poem No. 8

I can edit this novel forever
And feel no closer to finished
Because perfection is the snake
Gobbling its shaker
And isn't it true if we lose a limb
We endure its screaming phantom
Because ghosts are memories the stories
Repeat to themselves like the shells of
Humans
Strewn across the freeway
Because freedom is never free &
A penny earned is a hole burned
In my pockets
And it's a wonder I help turn
This monstrous ball bearing
With my own 2 feet—
Ah
I always liked Barney Rubble
B/c his stubble
Reminded me of a ring of
Chocolate milk.

11/21/21

Brown-napkin poem No. 9

Arms wide open into
A new day in America.
Caffeinated. Amped up.
Schools scratching the itch.
Stop & go. Red, green & yellow.
Bolivia. Lithuania. Congo.
We're really doing it. We've done it now.
Leaving ourselves behind.
A scrap. A line. Flesh recurring in dreams.
Genius nobodies 2-stepping among us.
The pull of city lights. The country's
Belly where our blood is buried.
Wanda Coleman haunted by Neruda
Whispering his name. Astral projections
For the birds. Splatter your insides onto
The page. Take my job. I'm halfway teasing.
Poems straddling you to the finish line
Shaped like threats. Do not feed the
Man with the pen—he, among the
Animals
Where the price is too high.

Brown-napkin poem No. 10

I dreamt it didn't hurt to be wrong
Just small—
Didn't look both ways &
Leveled on a parking lot
For Christ's sake—
Carson McCullers nursed me
With a soggy cinnamon-ringed
Deathstick—
William Carlos Williams checked my
Pulse & chanted poetically
Fine by me
Fine by me—
A danger to strangers
In the care of milky hands
I closed my eyes &
Counted 10 hens
Where between breaths
A knocking in my chest
(Don't open up)—
What results from pressing
The flesh cave in the center of
My body?—
I could've had anything I wished—
Hate & silence falling like leaves
Shielding my face from the city
Draped in sin & humility.

White-napkin poem No. 2

"I've heard of you," she said—
Because I've refused to hold captive
Those tongue-wrenching ideas.

Madness, like cancer,
From the inside
Out.

A release valve shaped like man.

A blade behaved as pen.

The up & down of your lover's sleeping
Chest as rain plays the windowpane.

There are moments
Words
Get the entire picture wrong.

Silence which buries
Everything worth remembering.

I saw a little girl draw w/ her pointer finger
A large smiley face in the dirt.
She seemed to take her work seriously.
Strangers stepped around it.

All things considered
We are also capable of this.

White-napkin poem No. 3

I dreamt I was a Bronze-Age
Detective in mind & spirit
And walked on the mud footprints
Leading away from the crime scene
And our feet were the same size
(a 10 by Nike standards)
And I couldn't gather proper psychic
Data cuz the stride was unremarkable
And before I knew it
Tho I saw it fleshing out
Like a movie
I fled the crime scene accused of
Pulling the faulty trigger
And I kicked off my shoes &
Recorded a voice-memo poem in which
Equality was real
(we could've been so much closer)
And justice was cashless—
I'd turn myself in out of
Duty & pride & O!
The unbridled reading time I'd buy
In exchange for freedom.

White-napkin poem No. 4

All we have is our body
Which is the voice & figure
Of the poem—
What doesn't kill us
Buys time for more records—
Might I suggest Coltrane?—
For valid reasons laughing is
Outta the question for some—
The canvas surrounding haikus
Haunts me as the air & water &
Light from which we feed—
To think prolonging death
And packaging it in a big bomb
Is our crowning achievement—
There's too much 2 grapple w/
In our free time—
Where to begin with something
So small & meaningful
As a book recommendation?—
Our bodies won't save us but
The musical voice sings on.

Gum-wrapper poem No. 26

With your bank account full
It's easy to stare down the sun &
Say, "I want to be your child."
If you can perform 100 pushups daily
It's easy for Vitality to ride you like
The final charge. W/ everything on
The line like an epic poem demanding
Our breath, how to sit still & not flail?

Brown-napkin poem No. 11

Learn the language

Its peculiar rhythms

Nothing's fixed

Not words tattooed on skin

Nas said you're heaven-sent

Not a metaphor for me

Funny papers framed w/ cheap desire

Pesos on the flimsy dollar

Sea-foam wings in vanilla sky

No-burn candles w/o time

Nice one, chief

This music won't bewitch itself

The overtorqued "I" in divine

I can change a tire but can I define the

Difference between unbelievable & un-

Deniable w/o breaking a few eggs for

The Omelette of the 4th Wall?

The period as a blink & a breath

The period as double dare to

Swallow that bullet on your tongue.

Gum-wrapper poem No. 27

The father knelt before his son
Who would grow into a poor poet
And asked the child w/ blazing eyes
"Are you lying to me?"
The truth would soon come
As the lonely heart pulls tears
Toward the worn soul.

Coffee-sleeve poem No. 7

The impact of all the words
I never left behind, the hands of two
Grandparents I held as they slipped
Into death
Which I hold this
Pen responsible for.

The coffee cools too soon.

The morning still beside me
In this poem
With no plans of leaving
For as long as I need.

Gum-wrapper poem No. 28

With the moon on
My back
My plight isn't
Langston Hughes'.
With plenty of rest
Still I'm pooped.
I mouth a white-
Lipped "todo bien"
To the moon riding
Me into the ground.
The dirt is winter-
Cold & sleep runs laps
Over my crown like a
Sheepdog w/ energy
To burn.

Gum-wrapper poem No. 29

The past is never dead
Faulkner said—if so
I'm still riding my bike
No destination in sight
Making promises to Grandma
To carry her to grocery
Stores when her legs give
Out—promises fleeting
As second lives. The
Wind still whips my face
Fills my throat w/ gnats
And lies. Pedal faster.
Dinner's an hour away.
Tomorrow never
Arrives.

1/26/22

Brown-napkin poem No. 12

Today is one of those days
In which every 5 minutes
I can drop my backpack & run.
From what? Surely not my fixed
Perspective—not the toxin inside
From which I mine these words
Nourishing & suffocating steadily.
A poet friend once penned himself
Out of death only to be locked in a
Page. All I have left of him:
His signature & a PDF document of
His last (unpublished) book
Which I cannot bring myself to finish.
I can hardly bring myself to escape
Though not once have I regretted
The decisions I've made
Which I made the best that I could.
The small joy of a water fountain
Drowning pretentious shoppers' chatter.
The simple pleasure of being asked to
Sign my book at a local bookstore.
What goes unread is the same as
What goes unsaid. (It goes w/o saying.)
The point of breath & noise is to enjoy
The total embrace of coming silence.
I will save dying for tomorrow.
For here & now, my ears are open.

Gum-wrapper poem No. 30

It is said cracked
Glass means the damage
Is already done. I
Have hugged my knees at
The risk of falling by
The wayside. Greed spins
Sermons despite my country's
Sins. Count me in. Turn
The soil. Turn the whole
Soul over. Cryptic.
Plato smirking at his
Bullshit. We're smaller
& louder. Here is what
I picture: babies in
A punk rock band.

White-napkin poem No. 5

When Alex Ebert sings
She got jumper cable lips
I understand the image because the women of
My page are perfect when—only when—
The darkness shuts my eyes.

Because sharp teeth. Electricity.

Shortages in the city.

A city's only a city
If car envy
Gasses our star.

Medina: suggestive in 3 tongues.

Income—then out you go.
How can one sit so still
But still
Be on the run?

(Do not buy a gun.)

Frightened & lonely in the city.
One among a cool million bleeding needles fueled by
Petrol rainbow pools.

In the city:
My truth vs. yours.

I read about our city from my library where each book
Is more dangerous than the last. How we got here is
A long & complicated story. I'm willing to believe
Angels will fall from the sky & sort our affairs so long as
My suspension of disbelief is supported by glass- & steel-
Coated cages obstructing my view of the plains where it is said
People of faith dance around a campfire.

The song of love & death in the city.
Can you hear me sing from the shower?
Only in this poem do I sound like Ritchie Valens.
The throat as a cracked runway. / The note as a
Rattling Beechcraft.

Invest in thy neighbors to the extent that they
Turbocharge thy unique simulation.

Duh.

If you've named/personified your vehicle—
Your lemon, your carriage, your chick magnet, your buggy, your bike—
Welcome to the city built just for us.

Stay on your side. Join my team. Come inside to apply.
No experience necessary! Stick around & the lies
Moisturize your skin to where everything slides off you
Like an irresponsible conviction in heavenly salvation.

There're only so many lives that can survive on this napkin.
Never mind that it's white.

All the better to witness our messes.

2/08/22

Receipt poem No. 1

James Joyce can't bother w/ me
2day. I can't bother w/ the
Super Bowl mañana. Curiosity
Killed our neighborhood cat but
It survives strutting on more
Lives. A snow-haired woman
Lugged w/ 1 arm a bag of
Trash bigger than her—I
Marveled, no 1 else around, at
True strength—what else have
I totally misread? In other
Words: I'm a weak man w/
Decent biceps. Like you, I
Hide well behind this body.
Inside: dynamite pretzeled
In2 a peace prize. We'll call
It poetry: an art so old
Even yo' mama can't
Recognize it.

Brown-napkin poem No. 13

I dreamt multiple realities danced between my
Fingers—I covered my eyes & counted to 10—
I heard the bombs sending souls to the
Sun in the Ukraine—I saw a storm cloud
Darker than rot—I prayed for Godzilla to
Rise again & fry the hydra inside men—
My prayer shot past God & I knew
We were doomed to solve the problem of saving
Ourselves in a cavernous classroom w/ a permanent
Substitute teacher—no blackboard—Lord
It's painful to sit so still when Chaos
Sings our names in dreams—we search for
Her even when we're awake—spread out on the battlefield
Howling like a battalion of lone wolves.

2/28/22

White-napkin poem No. 6

I thought by today
I'd have something more significant
To say—
Unbearable illiteracy rates
Creeps in suits & black robes
Legalese picking clean the bones
Love tainted & plucked from the
Collective tongue
The rising cost of grief therapy—
Nope—I bought a John Updike
Novel for 50 cents at a bookstore whose
Primary source of income comes from Magic
Cards—I gave the owner a dollar & said
"Keep the change"—Like I was
Doing her a
Favor.

Brown-napkin poem No. 14

"Get up from the floor, guy," a father chirps at his young son,
And I wonder if, years later, the boy, now a man,
Reads a tattered book from the ground, lying on his back,
An old book he found at an antiques shop, pure chance,
A nearly forgotten book his wife insists discovered him,
For when it comes to literature the relationship is one-
Directional, a river transporting the deeds and hopes &
Dreams setting us apart in the kingdom of God, so it is said,
And how effortlessly a book in the river's care becomes a
Smattering of cockled ink, and even that too changes, leaving us
With the fact of the river, the fragility of paper words, though
They live on mangled in our minds, fables battered by a game
Of Telephone, and I want to be able to recognize the book
The boy'll someday read, the book which swims its way to
Him—but I'm afraid this is one detail I cannot
Manage on this beautiful day, & so I'll carry it with me
In accordance with the laws of nature, which I am
Barely beginning to understand,
Let alone accept.

White-napkin poem No. 7

I have no opinion on
The people of the plains—
Road rage on the highways &
Rusted railways across the city
Cuz the country I recall is
Already gone like the fallen angels—
Good morning'll come & maybe my
Heart will brim in
Remembrance of that tender gesture:
Embrace—
The coffee'll be necessarily strong &
Enemies' enemies will conspire
Where the water drops & cools—
My opinion
Like the people
Changes with every step
And thus it's best
To remain silent
Like Wittgenstein
Whereof one cannot speak—
Although we know
Philosophers are the biggest bullshitters
This side of hell &
The Alamo.

03/29/22

White-napkin poem No. 7 ½

On the other hand

Wild Wild West still slaps.

03/29/22

Brown-napkin poem No. 15

To spit
On this napkin
In the kitchen
Of Death
Without audience
Nor applause
Is a show
Of endurance &
Foolishness &
Valor
No slain dragon
Can attest
And if even one
Accepts your head
As separate payment
Like John the Baptist's
Then you've won
This silly game
Like a book
On clearance
In the library
Of Babel
And that
Is enough—
That is enough.

4/12/22

Receipt poem No. 2

One man's trash is
Another scribe's literature—
True & untrue—
Christ rises today—
True & untrue—
Bloated rhyme
Moonwalks across the grave—
True & untrue—
My baby kin's giggle
Livens an emptied living room—
A missed joke atop my head
Summoning rain that never came—
True. True.

4/17/22

Campbell's Soup-can poem

No matter what condition
I'm in, Poetry stays open—
Mouth of a hollow soup can—
Spill secrets
Or sleep silent in bed—
Notice the
Difference
Anyway?

Brown-napkin poem No. 16

Another poet
Delivered to
The promised land
Which isn't promised
But dreamed—
By whom?—
The engaged citizens
So-called—
Engaged with what?—
Tripping wires &
Eating words
Which do not
Go down
Easy—
Very little is easy—
Words are easy
But they kill—
Life is easy
To let go
And it's over
Even as it
Unfolds
Like a bad hand
In Texas hold 'em—
Bluff 'em
Fool—
Let the sweat
Light up
Your face—
Laugh now &
Do the math
Later—
Alligator—
Terminator—
Gone, goodnight
Tom Keene—
Promise to save me
A seat
Wherever you are
On the road—
At the table of
Poetry
Where Kerouac
And Sappho

Dipped out
To pick a bone
With Confucius—
I'm still digesting
Eve's apple
Here in the
Motherland—
Wonderland Mall—
The best of
San Antonio—
The worst of
Putting up your guard—
My pen slipped
And painted my wrist—
A finite line
On a finite body
Part man part lie—
Parlay—
This game—
The smoke in my
Throat—
Who put it there
Or did I
Do that?—
Who put you there?—
Or did I do that?—
Do you trust a
Poet in cahoots
With Death?—
How many questions
Does it take to
Get to the center
Of a Tootsie Pop?—
2 much is sacred
And 2 much is
Drywall—
A poor man's fort—
My forte—
Losing steam—
Catching up to my
Ghost—
There is nothing left
To explain.

White-napkin poem No. 8

The edge of the world glowing
On this poem about the dash
To nowhere—
So much left to do
So much left to forget
Like Tim Seibles
I shout
Fuck Death!—
Eyes sunk like robbers in a tomb
Searching for the perfect word—
The cave that loves me back—
Limbs intact & conscience sprinting to
The edge of the glowing world
Beyond the poem / beyond the zero
To a cave loving me back—
Swallow the dark & spend a life
Losing the light you thought bright.

4/21/22

Poem from a leather notepad gifted from one writer to another to another

The air not quite real—stay put there.
The books won't read themselves.
Nor can you cure desire. Provenance.
Penny thoughts & slow-burn
Vanilla aroma—
"There is color in my life, but I'm not
Aware of any structure."
If somebody instructs you
What a real writer is
They are not real. Change:
The nature of reality—
Tiresome game—word playing the
Tongue like Santana's air guitar.
To fall in love with being wrong.
To stuff one's veins with sugar
And wager sweet dreams.
No good. No good.

4/25/22

Notepad poem

You said to write a poem
About you—so I look into
Your third eye & say
This will have to do—
Has a slice of the cosmos
Always been around your
Neck?—
That is my sister,
You say, but this is my
Voice—in some ways
2 big for Texas like every-
One else here—footprints on sand—
There is an art studio
Built on the bones of love
And science, & the artist
Sells her tears—it is 2
Treacherous & beautiful to
Put a price on them—but
The artist must eat—the father
Must be remembered as a dream—
How do you wear the stars around
Your throat? I ask—
They are not for sale, you say,
But I am listening.

4/26/22

Notepad poem No. 2

I.

10 years ago
I told the story of a girl
Whose bones were
Failing her

And when they did
I couldn't find the story
And since then
The newspaper has yellowed
In a box in my head.

II.

The story really happened
And the girl's family thanked me
And I shot my grief at God
Whose property must be riddled
With bullet holes
In the shape of His imagination.

III.

The story isn't really mine
But she was bald & precious
And we're supposed to say
Thank you, God, for this
Cruel world
In the shape of your imagination?

IV.

Every poem I write
Belongs to me more than
You think
But take them away—
I cannot love them
Equally
Which is a sign of a
Good father
With a bad heart
In the shape of
God's fist—

Revolution is for
Children—
Democracy injured
On the bed of romantics—
Democracy stripped bare
In the waiting room of the
Desert where our dead
Await instruction
From a body of light.

V.

This is my poem—
My life—not my
Life—my story
Finished by you.

White-napkin poem No. 9

A pink Minnie Mouse chair
Beneath the freeway
Where I expect a beaten face
To be   there—
My gaze hopping across
The maze of
Scheduled distraction—
From what?—you know what—
Loose change in my pocket
Not that it benefits any
Lost cause—I'm seated here
But not on that pink chair &
The money light disappears
This poem   here.

5/01/22

Gum-wrapper poem No. 31

Loose hair snipped from the beard of a reading slump
like: That which is within is 2 much to bear—the music
still distracts, the problem's your ears, the moral silence of
changing seasons—100-degree heat in San Antone means my
favorite low-key bookshop's a sauna of waning thought—
Houston, we have a problem, from this altitude, a bad
attitude away from liftoff—you mean the moon? the host
that hypnotized Oswald before he lit this country up?—
yes, a flag's a mask, like a poem wears (down) the
poet—chew the lies, then you might find the kernel of
truth—won't go down smooth—but all the cool kids
are doing it.

5/7/22

Tic Tac poem

Photographer watching
us frolic across that
green frame like
wishes lost at sea—
the bad breath that
made this love real—
the soul in flux—it's
alive—I swear, alive.

White-napkin poem No. 10

A man in a Ghostface tee
Chaperones his daughter
Dressed in pink to the restroom
And she couldn't be happier,
Not to me, not on this Sunday w/
Temperature & gas prices tearing thru
The record-book roof,
A hole in the soul another kind of
Smiling mouth wrangling its words
Carefully, partner,
For the fabric needs good patchin'—
To my right, Fauci's book titled
Expect the Unexpected—
Yes, the aphorisms will save us,
And when the weather freezes over
In hell
The white coats will wrap us in
White coats &
We'll march down that path single file,
Someone's drum, inner voices,
A child asking her father:
Where are we going, Daddy?
When will we get there?

5/15/22

Gum-wrapper poem No. 32

Smiley face on the flush button /
Audacity of a tiny midday revolution
From the wound-tip of a Sharpie /
Somedays the hand moves as it may /
Mayday mayday the Monday flower
Galaxy makes its own rules / we, of
Same mind, scruples / baby doomers /
Start w/ the good news.

5/16/22

Post-it Note poem

So I told that slow learner (me):
Justice ain't just!
A hug is xtra heat &
The white Mustang on fire on
The streets—dissension in
The chamber / pressure between
The sheets—a blanket:
The heart's second skin—
The heart: God on the breath—
What beauty we've cooked up—
Burning stories in the sky,
The eyes: what terrible vision,
What tears left untold.

Brown-napkin poem No. 17

Coffee run turned into a
"Johnny Depp | Amber Turd"
Tip jar & guess which horse I
Bet my chips on—oh geez, shoulda
Known nothing in life's free,
Not even yuks & O yuck!
Another book festival out there
In the southern oven when every
Day's a book festival in my home,
My mind which isn't to be conflated
With brain or flesh more or less
Accounted for & justified by
Atomic leapfrogging & oh my, how does
He get from here to there? Pay me
And the recipe's yours—paint me
And methinks I need new robes—
Oh God, serviettes outta service are
Good for what?—fractured narratives are
Corrupt cops—"the heat is real hot,"
A young father heat-advises his young daughter—
Welcome to the festival where your intellect's
Up for grabs but please don't touch me—
Let me brood in peace: a complete sentence
Lacking sense like the bodies we're baked in—
If you have to ask, I say:
You're more than ready to find out.

5/21/22

Brown-napkin poem No. 18

The kids.
Eyes & skin
Beautiful but
Nothing fits.
This napkin.
Toss it.
So young &
Hurting
Here.
No terms w/
Uncertainty. Fear.
At the table.
Kick the legs out
From under our chairs.
To crawl again
Where it begins.
We'll do it. We'll win.
But man—
Nothing fits.

5/25/22

White-napkin poem No. 11

I met a traveller from an antique land
And her name was sandpaper
And her body was dead sea—
What're you eating? I asked,
A fish? a serpent?
It's not good, she said,
But it's mine, & so I can
Speak—
Wrecked, I went home
And discovered my
Words were silent—
My books were missing—
I tried painting on
A new tongue
But all it did
Was ruin
My teeth.

6/1/22

White-napkin poem No. 12

I dreamt faith &
Reason combusted in
The clouds & under-
Ground & doves
Shat on our dreams
And poetry transported
Us but didn't save
Us & the pews were
Empty & the loveseats
Were empty & the
Great books were flat
Ideas like a late-Picasso
Nightmare & the pen
In my hand was a glove
And the hand on my arm
Was a cactus & the
Silence was sound & the
Trees were toy chests
And God was a fleet of angels—
A ring in the bloody sky—
And the wedding lasted 8 nights—
So many hearts were fed—ears wept
And nobody slept a lick.

6/6/22

White-napkin poem No. 13

I, the past present writing into the future.
What is the future but the past propelled?
What is the present but the future melting
In my dead palms? Is it each of us carrying
3 clocks going up on an escalator
Down in an elevator
Lying down looking up crushing time
On our backs—put the I on its side
And the 2 endpoints signify the beauty, baby,
And horror of parallel inescapability
Which is to say linguistically I am not
Alone—but damn, where'd everybody
Go? It's not that it's lonely at the top
But the birds & lightning are bad at
Telling jokes & when I say "knock knock"
I find that it's me on the other side of
The door—there's a tome in my hand
In case nobody answers. Planning ahead—
A hydra head of presence.
Knock knock—I'm already
Home.

6/8/22

Gum-wrapper poem No. 33

What brings you to your knees.
What demons you kill.
What kills you.
A human.

6/9/22

Notepad poem No. 3

I dreamt I was a corn cob pipe dream
And how I developed my tired politics
Slapdash style & hack humor
Was beyond words / just out of reach
Like a duck half a step slow
Like being similar & not even close
Like as not / not as like those
Packed so tight in feelings
Everyplace I (don't) know
Even the desert reeks of tears
Bleeding from all 5 senses like
Mario Santiago Papasquiaro, like
A homesick child wrecked w/ fear
And where do we go from here?
Mother Teresa said every dream precedes the goal
And that's it, this dream never ends because
Death is temporary & pain is forever
But hey, how about a joke—
A math book slumps into a doctor's office
And grumbles "I've got problems, man" &
Doc says "I see, but I'm only a dentist"—
Even math books carry teeth
You learn something new everyday
The sunshine & moonlight in tiny victories
We need only an inch / balled up so long in armor
I forget how tall you really are
Ain't that something? Hey, ready for another joke?
Just kidding—skidding down the pipe
Our souls on trial scratching the surface of
Trash—the writing is dead
Always has been
Which means we're forgiven
The sin of living w/ abandon
And if this isn't a poem
Then I'm not a mouth
Biting down hard on my
Heart on fire—my
Tongue be like, "Be cool."

6/10/22

Water-bottle-cap poem

① We work for the blurbs, we write to the writers.
② We die for you & the blue ache ain't hurt so true.

Brown-napkin poem No. 19

Dear reader, ever tried spying
The cupboards for answers
Or the bottom of your feet
Your filthy soles? :)
C'mon, man—you're not searching soul
Searching hard enough—think about it
Consult the library look around skip around
Circle back to me on the half-
Life of sensibility—you want a true story?
There's a rogue fighter pilot in my blood
Stream scourging villainy & testing the
Waters of justice in the dry environs of
South Texas but only after midnight—
There's a homeless fella in Houston who threw
A chocolate chip cookie at my face as well as
A safe life—I've met the ghost of
Philip K. Dick in a café in a shopping mall
And that guy's a … well his books are
Cool meaning I am the ass doomed to a
Brain but OK & your excuse
Being?

6/14/22

Post-it Note poem No. 2

I dreamt I saw Poetry with
People of the night & went with it
My car having broke down &
My legs sailing second wind—
Like Allen Ginsberg I spotted
Walt Whitman poking around the
Supermarket & when I moseyed over
Every ripe tomato held the sad
Vision of death like Dickinson
Weeping Moctezuma's tears &
I looked down & found my Air Force 1s
Missing—feet long & narrow like a
Crepe myrtle scratching on heaven's door
Falling short & loud like a proud child—
Even your favorite kicks don't carry you home.

6/16/22

Paper-towel poem

Where'd my personal story-time shag carpet go?
Where'd the pre-millenium hand-smashing iron go?
Where'd the driveway buzzer beaters go?
The wayward front-lawn palm tree?
Hot & humid ecosystems / millions of oil particles
Dotting our lungs into ladybugs. O horrid manners
Slingshot acorns snapped skateboards chunked into
Weedy ditches sunflower seeds sprouting anywhere
O the Oz-green grass wet, dry & like the lives
We knee-slid into the blood like ketchup &
Swimming pool bottoms teasing at sky infinity
You ain't seen a cannonball like mine get so
Thoroughly erased by jelly / in my left hand a
Barking dog / in my right the sign of the cross
My first crush blonde & unattainable thank God for
Uphill-battle climbs I require only a sip of
Drip a camel chewing bitterness & iron he's too
Proud to spit out / on one hand growing up
The other walking a tightrope buried under sand
Understand if you've tossed a jellyfish back at sea
We can be friends—I'm not anything like you
But let's us 2 bottle up your courage call it
Nobility / sunburnt genies cleaning up trash at
The beach—O the painful peeling later
Layers of ghost stories in your hands
What does love taste like to you?
Full-blooded post-sneeze euphoria
I'll take seconds, please. Thank you!

6/17/22

Gum-wrapper poem No. 34

Abandoned detective story
in a folder, folder in a
rubbish bin, my pen awfully
maudlin, parrot in a paper
dungeon, collection of
explosions & this kindling of
flesh & bone could've been so
many dreams—I dreamt
I growled into a microphone
mourning the loss of everything
& cowboys in the crowd gave
me a standing O, as in they
rated my performance a zero
and I stood beside
Katherine Anne Porter in
the buffet line awaiting
cardboard steak, a smack
in the face—they won't soon
forget mine. Right?

6/20/22

Gum-wrapper haiku

Nothing to king to
Ashes, three homes—no will. Hey
Papa, you laughing?

6/21/22

Bookmark haiku

Mother's eyes, power
I'll never see—your sunrise
Laugh, best part of me.

6/22/22

Page-ripped-from-a-book poem

I dreamt I was approaching the end of the dream—
33 steps in, long but soon forgotten like years, my
Father's eyes, my mother's smile (& ears), Grand-
Father's legs and Grandma's cast-iron will pushing me
Past weeds and beach shells cutting my heels,
The hurt isn't nice but it's right, I see the writing in
The sky, that blue ghost I know, beautiful stars
Around its neck, Vonnegut's words in my grip,
You've gotta fling that death wish out there, someone's
Chambers, someone's waiting room, the books are all
Lying to you, the dream's almost thru, Tumbleweed Drive
To tumbleweed sprint across the plains of delivery
And graves, the water lapping at your feet, the
Wounds nice but not right, they're mine & yours
Inching toward the illusion of a great dividing line—
I dreamt I approached the end of the dream &
My pages trailed behind like neglected offspring
And someday they'd make me pay, but not yet, today,
Heroes letting me down & I retelling their tales of
Nightmares and runaway loves, we should've seized
The light, it's not too late, right, to fall down &
Grow up again? the dream is ending but I hold back
These tears, welcome the sun & moon for new songs
They sing, I'm listening, my pen is ready—yes,
Happy to scratch fresh legends into the dirt, the
Harvest, the earth your heart brushing against my
Cheek, a million birthday wishes—a soft kiss
For each that comes true.

6/23/22

Brown-napkin poem No. 20

Heat dome—
You should see my finances, tho!
Only the necessities, book stacks
Growing to the ceiling ... up high, Jack—clap clap
"God, why didn't they close her eyes?"
Remarked my mom upon seeing Frida's
Black-n-white corpse at the end of the
Painful documentary—she's told me time
And again she doesn't want to burden
Us in the end—& then she showed me old
Family photos—beautiful and painful—
My mind isn't w/ this poem but somewhere
In Italy, dreaming in a Spanish tongue
Lost—a thunderstorm won't stop
The heat to come—is love present or is it
Already gone?
That bittersweet waiting
For night.

White-napkin poem No. 14

On this 6th day of September 2022,
$2.55 burrowing its way to my wallet
(Poetry royalties)
I nest here unregal
Supremely regaled by 2 dead white authors
In my bone-dry vise-grip
Pondering dead words left
Inside the tank
And how anyone cares about anything—
Zoom out: ah! the baton twirlers
In a kind of beautiful living hell
And try as I might to hopscotch galaxies
I awake to the same dream
Return to the same red smile (lovely)
Filling my half-gone Pixie cup w/ water
For I am thirsty and thrive in a circular
Garden filled w/ infinite ideas & madness &
The promise of tomorrow—
A gleam in your green underground eyes—
It speaks in your tongue &
It was home long before you arrived.

Coffee-sleeve poem No. 8

On paper
Our lives can be weighed
In coffee sleeves.
Sunday morning &
All's quiet for the time
Being. Sheesh.
Einstein, that you wrapped round my
Wrist? Why, this lease of flesh?
Perpetually late wherever it's supposed
To go.

10/9/22

Post-it Note-folded-hotdog-style poem

I was a bookmark
for one day then
trash folded in the
panache of hotdogs
an American pastime
invented by Germans
but do folks(tales) invent
food? Yeah that's called
scribing yourself into a
corner flytrap labyrinth
like that one flick w/
Nicholson whose snow
Face is all 2 familiar—
a ghost wielding an ax
wearing a smile you swore
yesterday had your best
interests at heart.

10/11/22

White-napkin poem No. 15

Often we are gifted
more space than we know what
to do with and so I opt for
my meager slice with grace &
delight—how the open palette
of the casino in the inhospitable
section of our soul is so calculated
as to be trife—it is always today
today and when Christ said the meek
will inherit the earth did he mean
the living or the dead?—what's a life
good for if not to learn anything the hard
way?—death always plays for an audience of one.

10/17/22

White-napkin poem No. 16

Often we are
gifted too much
time and so
I say
two-a-days!
If a clown
from the clouds
told you to
follow the twisting
rain would you
open up &
drink from the
gray chalice of
mystery's heart?
I heard a
man say today
"What's up, chief?"
and the sky
opened up its
curtains and revealed
its all-star
brass section—
another kind of
electroshock
therapy—therapy—
a word that
reeks of anti-
septics &
closed-book
energy like the
tales of old—
gold chariots
in the mouths
of monstrous
birds like dreams
like broken-winged
visions in the
hands of Langston
Hughes &
hues so bright
like lemons in
the eyes of
our dead
and I

want to
keep going
I want
to keep
going
stop &
Listen
I can't
keep
going
where
have
I gone?

10/17/22

White-napkin poem No. 17

Urgency
as in reverse verse
is a breed of
boredom—
I didn't look at the
young blond homeless man
in a white & pink Spurs cap
but I read his cardboard—
urgency as non-contact—
and when the poet Elisa Gabbert
poeted that we remember our hotel
room #s only to forget 'em forever
it's cuz emergency's left our bodies cool
like the chill of unshakeable death
before our sun presides back behind
the heavy curtains of Oz and shines
on us so brightly it's almost perfect—
for a sec—
like shutting your eyes &
the heavy souls who helped carry you
here whisper exactly
what you wanna
hear
here.

10/20/22

McDonald's coffee-cup poem No. 2

```
    r           b
    e           e
    a           h
    l           i
    i           n
    t           d
    y     I

M   c     C   a     f   é
a   o     a   n     a   t
n   m     n   d     c   e
i   e               e   r
c   s     h   s         n
          a   o     t   a
t   t     r         h   l
h   h     d   I     a   l
e   e     l         t   y
          y
    w           f   m
    o     h     a   i
    r     i     c   n
    d     d     e   e.
    s     e
```

10/21/22

Plastic-cup poem

I want to talk about Kanye
West's "Flashing Lights"—that
Spike Jonze music video—the
death of the ego in a tuxedo
at the hands of an assassin
in lingerie—side ass?—the
death yelp in the desert silenced
by gag & groove and that old blinding
shift in culture—that dance in
the mirror so sleazy—but what
do you know, Alex? Your eyes are
on fire & you will be held account-
able able-bodied like as not that
warning label to start—do your
pages change the horror of memory
the shovel that will bury you the
loveflame of real women the old subtle
tremor in culture the trembling
hearts of real men the
cycle of disappearance?

10/22/22

White-napkin poem No. 18

I wanna talk a lil' more bout
Ye's "Flashing Lights" cuz I wasn't
done (space restrictions) and I am the
eye on fire behind the white curtain
sunglasses always dying &
always reviving like the Terminator—
yes, the killer behind the fake flesh as I am
the soul behind the cold prose & West the hot
note behind the man behind the monster
endless night—O how many times I've
heard friends recite "Fuck Kanye" and I'm
like, Hey, some attacks are personal
but all are vital—hey, are we all not
merging into that abyss day by night?
Salinas, could it be you're showing off
(I never thought you would take it this far)
boy this ain't nothing they don't already know—
like Artaud's theater of cruelty everything is
truth—light & base & shock & shadow.

10/23/22

White-napkin poem No. 19

When the poet Franz Wright said
"There is only one heart in my body, have mercy
on me"
And my heart stopped—
Today the sky the most brilliant of blues
And blue, too, my mind, grass in the shadows,
Books as broken lives left behind, have mercy
on me—you can age yourself out of this
World but not your thoughts, the calling
Cards of folks you can't call back,
Is it plausible you could've done no better?
I made the storm move with me, O Lord,
Thank you for letting me fear your Love, have
Mercy.

10/25/22

Gum-wrapper poem No. 35

To walk into a meeting late
4 stories closer to God after someone's
stress-cry painted the sky the dye of
childhood home on a street named after
tumbleweeds where there were none—
not everyone likes to laugh the same as
flaws lengthen like nails and the trees
harbor (seemingly) secrets like poems set ablaze.

10/26/22

White-napkin poem No. 20

That's it—it's taken me 20
white napkins to understand
again
the perfect poem does not exist
here
because it lives (for now) in our hearts
(unwritten) only for us
to survive
and so this insane chase must ensue—
but damn
the illusive motions have meant
so much
like a simple flip of the red hair,
your scent on me in the cinema
dark till the end of dreams
which I misplace again &
again
and so the chase resurrected
under the watch of dying stars
and the "I" trying so hard to leave
its body behind like a foolish monk
with iron fists or the crucifix
buried in a drawer—
force majeure—
I don't wanna chase you anymore
but off the page you flee into the green
so what am I supposed to do,
sit here and think?

10/27/22

Half Price Books price-tag haiku

Signed Kinky
Friedman half
price? Holler!
In October
Christ
mas
played.

10/29/22

Hershey's wrapper poem

W/o a manuscript, shopping for a publisher
Is like looking for God in your hair—
It could work! Like Borges, are we
Capable of all ideas? I was told this
Is a terrifying idea. I told myself last
Year "I want no more to be a man—only
Green grass." Methinks that was a bad
Idea. A bite of chocolate hardly seems
Enough. It is. It gave me
This. Whatever this is.

11/4/22

Gum-wrapper poem No. 36

I'm a poet; I
just write things.
4 p.m. on a Friday
staring at what
appears to be a halo
above a rooftop
under which lies
love & suffering so
intertwined even the
walls just shut up.
I've lived this day b4.
I'm strong & still as a
rock. I push myself
up hills. I wave at clocks.

Gum-wrapper poem No. 37

Will I, the mortal gaze, be thru soon
talking about KW's "Flashing
Lights"? I'm sorry—you cannot
negate a haunt. What changed is
nothing—the scapegoat skin
fastened tight & gaunt. Were you there
among my contemporaries? Drunk every
word you spilled? The desert was an ocean.
The ocean a dark thrill.

Coffee-lid poem

A friend & retired
scholar once told me
to recapture the missing
tongue from my
tongue. I said, "And why
didn't you learn Yiddish?" As
if our 50-year age gap
were reconciled by the
bottom of an empty
coffee cup.
"It is an otherwise dead language," he said—and I knew then that healthy distance was a
virtue—death our 3rd
wheel & referee.

White-napkin poem No. 21

I once nearly attempted the Great American Poem on a fallen leaf but good grief is nothing sacred? I once talked myself off the ledge by diving into the deep end head first & my nose is still burning and my eyes are still closed. I once hugged my grieving older brother so hard I lost myself in the world & was a gold spoon on a silver-tongued forked path. I once spilled my guts on an egg-white napkin but ate the napkin—you'll never get that close. I once promised my grandmother I'd take care of her for the rest of her life & in the end we faded with her in the fog in her mind. I once held my mom & we cried & afterward we laughed at everything & for a moment everything was so bright. I once wrestled my dad & dislocated his jaw and when he tells the story it never loses its humor & vitality. I once shared a few minutes alone w/ my little bro on his wedding day & only now do I have the urge to burst w/ pride. I once told my lover I'd love her forever & I knew that was proof that inside me God breathed. I once abandoned the novel I needed to write & wrote the one I wanted to write. (Come hither all ye slippery agents!) I once sacrificed my sanctity to poetry w/ a 1,001 conditions. I once was so blown away by books that I hoarded them & built a fort that's currently for sale. I once saw Danger Mouse in concert while my heart was a broken bell. I once thought strength resided in an 85-pound dumbbell. I once dreamt I went to hell w/ no hands & a 30-second memory. I dreamt my words saved my soul & I haven't woken up.

Notepad poem No. 4

This is not an endorsement—it's self-inflicted
tunnel vision. God, how some books are on
fire. We were driving down Wurzbach during
the witching hour when she said James
Cain's *The Postman Always Rings Twice* was written
in gasoline. I said, "Yes, and nothing is left
of that world." I have secrets not even
Death will pry out of me. I seized this pen
only because my nerve endings tingled—the shark
is swimming thru my heart. The difference between
prose & poetry is the brash moon or the shy host
on the Black Spandex. I was born to die
in myself. I live to exhaust extant ink
under my feet which do not always carry me home.
I own the words that own me. The letdown
is that people fill in their ghosts like Magritte's
Pilgrim. The letdown is that legends are boiled
into words. (This is a good problem to have.)
Some of my gasoline lives in a Nike shoebox;
I wear a 10 when I'm not fleeing from my life.
The last night of the Earth means it's still
night. Whether you die or not, always hit 'em with,
"Cool invite." When Frida said, "I hope the exit is
joyful," & left us w/ her appetite. I'm here for it. I
am part blind but my wings work just fine. Coming? Alright.

Water-lid poem

Clarity is the cyclops
and the hydra. To write is
to collide into the mirror.
To write is to die on
your own dime. (But
who are you trying to van-
quish?) The chances are extraordinary.
When all is sky-blue, build your
own monster. This is not a
literary   device.
A literal   devil.
A   tear.
A   leap.

11/8/22

Brown-napkin poem No. 21

It is probably true that since I've
tucked books under my arm
I have felt less alone.
I have read poetry walking to check
the mail at night &
I can't seem to glide slow enough
as if I had time under my control.
I saw a moth the size of a baby's fist
resting on my door and that was when
this poem was born.
If poems are all around us, even under
the floor, are we not already done for?
Hey, I'm watching *The Northman* &
the scenes are stark & silly but the
poetry's gorgeous. Why is it that I
always need to gorge on more focus? Is
this is even a poem? Can I hire the
form to seduce the rhythm? What a
blue question—what a crude jam session.
I, the guru of the lost. The music is pure
shine & gloss.

Brown-napkin poem No. 22

Back so soon again. 22. Cyndi Lauper's "Time
After Time" having a mysterious impact on the
impassable faces of my city's most splintered.
The language wraps itself around me again. The
cocoon of close but not close enough. I
told the bookstore manager, "Do you ever
look around and think, 'I don't want to
read most of this trash?'" Can you believe it?
I need to get my heart checked. By the way,
the manager said, "Yes." Sometimes it
seems as though I'm one giant shoulder to
lean on. That is someone's fantasy—&
I conjure them here. Twitter, you emotional
rag, you diary in a trash bag. I swear, the
other day I looked at the mirror & said,
"You're done," like De Niro. The mirror nodded
and blinked, like me. Back so soon again. Lord,
give me another shot & I'll return. The
sequels brought me here. The screaming child.
The future w/ eyes wide shut. The hooded slacker
walking out of my poem. The relentless
day does not call in sick. Sway. Let us pray.

White-napkin poem No. 22

This BIC Atlantis has dragged me places, man.
Nestled me & shut the blinds—(oh, it's
that kinda date?)—skirted my 3rd eye
(the only vision that binds) straight from the
grave of Georges Bataille—flicked the lights
off & on & yes—time for the final take on
Ye's "Flashing Lights"—how there are 2 many
star(killers) to count & the Night (that
journey) the frigid rule—I worry & hurt
for you—seen this show peering up from the
bottom of the blackbottom pool—(attached to
the mermaid, guide me home, Missile Muse)—
there's nowhere as far as the dark gallery of
your heart—let me in—waltz me out—in
my mouth a pilfered meteorite—slash in the
pan—the desert's soul—antique rug buried in
the billionth hole—
rigged rigmarole of burnt bridges—song
on repeat till I perish or cherish the Angel
of Death—a "Powered by Bitchdust"
bumper sticker on the old pickup truck—
I don't suppose you're 3 handfuls
of double trouble?—chief
chieftain Robert Parish swingin'
for the win—the good green
westward grin full of
heaven & sin—spin
this venom—wire of
blood thru the
chin.

11/9/22

White-napkin poem No. 23

Man, I've dragged this BIC Atlantis places.
The pen wouldn't leave me out of it, wasn't
having it, today. I feel strangely called to
forgive my legion of enemies imaginary & half
real. But that's because I'm seated &
my gaze is gravity-bent. Now I see Sylvia
Plath on the wall & can't imagine she'd
be thrilled. My friend, the poet
Aaron Rudolph, is addicted to penning trash
poems & sorry, brotha, but I'm
thrilled. After 2 mighty swats a
gnat replanted on my bicep—it just wants
to make friends. Half the time, the natural
world is that way. Right? Lord, thank
you for putting me back in. Letting me play
the game my way.

Monthly billing statement poem

My grandfathers shared exactly
one
story with me about their
time in the Army—one when
I was too young to die & the other
when I knew the score, like
El Greco. They're all gone now.
Ain't that something? I
wish my poems were like that.
They will be. Soon enough. Salute.

11/11/22

Gum-wrapper poem No. 38

Death our best editor. No words
a kind of noise. A dance partner
on fire. A tongue like kryptonite in a bottle.

Gum-wrapper poem No. 39

The woman
knitting at the
table
      alone
is a thousand years
of concentration.
Is eyes closed—
mask over her
nose. My age
asleep &
everything this
pen tries to be.

Notepad poem No. 5

You could get so close to
a grand old painting
you might get lost
on the other side—
you could touch nose to
nose with old pigments
& still look up
from under the stormy sea
with eyes from the bold fathers
and a body like an island
scattered with fruit
from a thousand trees—
are you trying to
dash the last stroke?—
becoming the master in front of
an audience of one?—
you're like the tweed coat
draped on a chair—
belonging to nobody—
no ghost
has looked so fine.

Gum-wrapper poem No. 40

Dave Brubeck, take 5—you are alive and well—
pull down the sky for me, the
colossal eyelid is heavy. From here
the Tower of Americas is a thumbnail
& baby, I'm no god—I'm no good
but I love what you've done, Lord. Move
me like a cursor, like a piano—somewhere
to call home—to fill a soul. Somewhere to flow.

Brown-bag poem

There's no such thing as a free poem.
Ha! I've long wanted to get that out.
Something has troubled me lately
and it is this: my last grandma saw her pa
in my face, which she held in her frail
grip like a pail of holy water—
my hairline and white tips the
spitting image of a paterfamilia I never knew
but whose shell I've grown into.
She did the sign of the cross and I
crossed my legs and tried to finish
my barbecue in good faith. Do I
believe in ghosts? When I was just past
the point of sacrificing my soul to literature
and just before the point at smashing my
head against a brick wall, I saw Roberto
Bolaño assuage me: "It's alright, fly under
my wings," and his leather jacket became
the permanent night and the silver pen my bleeding heart—
my sword, my flight—there is nothing I write
you can kill me with. Here, I'm already dead.
I mean this in good faith—there's no such
thing as a free life. Usher me from room to room
like a true host. Break bread to Nat King Cole. Rest
my head on the bed of your breast. Thread—the
thin red thread.

Gum-wrapper poem No. 41

On yesterday's
gum wrapper, I suppose
this is my alternative
exercise to cold
weather. I suppose
you think this
exorcise is me. Sadly
& righteously I am
the limitations of
my tongue, my dry
lips, as is language's
wont. I languish b4
I flaunt. I, the rib
b4 the breath—the
song strung to death.

White-napkin poem No. 24

Nov. 20, 2022. Pete Rock &
CL Smooth, help me reminisce, be
my Muse. This doesn't leave the
driveway. Pulling up for a jumper,
legs dead as this lead, he pulls up
in his pickup truck, skin raw &
whitened like dried milk on America's
bones. 15 years old—room in my
heart for Peja & Manu, training
lil bro & Linkin Park. "Wanna
shoot?" He's got on steel-toe boots, for
Pete's sake. "Okay." Slower these
days but stronger in a way. "I'll stand
under the rim and you ram me." He
chopped my arms in 2 like a Shaolin
monk. "You fouled me!" No, boy—not
then, not ever. "You take hacks from me,
you can take 'em from anyone." Didn't
become a man yet, those battles outside the
lines. My forearm scar not from him
but wish it were otherwise. Basketball
claimed my knees but left me poetry.
Dad still somewhere playing dirty, God
swallowing the whistle. 64 years wears you
well, old sport. Happy birthday, Pops.
Happy birthday, old world.

Brown-napkin poem No. 23

Playing for keeps on trash.
It's not the metaphor that keeps
me coming back.
Just because there's space
doesn't mean you have to take it!
Just because you take it
doesn't make it yours.
If you redefine your face every fortnight
you are toying with time on time's terms.
Does the metaphor keep us forthright
or are all words lies in comparison to
the images stuck inside like the blood
of which it seems there is often too much?
What have I really said?
You know me as well as this ink stays
alive & by and by that's not reliable!
Only fools leave notes open to interpretation.
Talking turkey—can someone explain that to me?

11/21/22

McDonald's coffee-cup poem No. 3

1.

```
                    t
                    o

        f           t
        e           h
        e           e
        l
        s           c           c
                    o           o
        o           r           l
        n           e.          d

        a           O           &
                    k
M       c       C   a       f   é
a       o       u   y.      o   p
n       f       p,          r   h
a       f                   g   e
g       e       m           e   m
e       e       a           t   e
                n!              r

y                           i   a
o               G           t.  l
u               e
r               t               w
                                i
                                n
                                d.
```

2.

Is a perfect
circle everything in
its somethingness or
nothing in a vacuum
of everything? Don't
touch anything—so,
nothing? Can nothing
be loved by
anything in the
nothing? There's
nothing to do about

anything. Even
dead is something.
Nothing is nobody
to me.

3.

Everybody is nobody
to nothing. Jeez!

11/22/22

Receipt poem No. 3

Nov. 24, 2022. The Land
is as quaint & industrial as
I thought, the denizens more
chatty (in a pleasant way) than
anticipated. Nearby my hotel,
there's a large wooden landmark
entitled (but not really) "Chief
Netawatwees Statue," and to
think I have open on my browser
a photo of Sherwood Anderson,
whose hard mouth half-dollar stone
eyes leave me feeling, quite frankly,
a visitor in a strange land—which
I am. And to think this is written
on a frozen custard receipt. It's
healthy to recall (is that the right
word?) that b4 anyone else got here,
there were more than 100 million
denizens here—b4 anyone else got
here—like time (a concept) long gone.
Salinas, let's not go there. It's a
beautiful day. The wings of the gods
as dreamt by mirrors got you here,
alive. Wanna know the kinda guy I
am? The first thing I said to the
Ohio sky was, "Sup, LeBron!" Yep.
As luck would have it, that kinda guy.

Snack Mix poem

The better question
is, is trash classy?
If I could trust a word as soon as it's
jotted down, things would be different.
I dreamt that form negates truth
& I   spent an hour arguing this
with Virginia Woolf on the plane.
She left impossibly energized and I never
heard from her again. Us writers were so
much more than our surface-level tension
works but compared to anything
it didn't mean a damn thing. Damn-near invisible.

White-napkin poem 25

Quivering quarters quartering quails.
Quails quartering quarters quivering.
Quarter-quails quivering quartering.
Quarter-quivering quails quartering.
Quarters quivering quail-quartering.
Quartering quivering quail quarters.
Quarter-quartering—quivering quails.
Quivering quail-quarters—quartering?
(You get the picture.)
P.S. I'm quivering kicking a cold.

11/27/22

Receipt poem No. 4

The garden, the arena, the livingroom.
The canvas, the prison, the map.
My life is dripping from my
nose, my eye is searching for
the strings—Return Policy: the body
may be returned once per
lifetime but the soul is
just another word for soiling
life onto the page—a sort
of shortsighted (or in-
complete) immortality. Each
day I scrape reality from my
gaze and I couldn't define
"real" for you if I tried. All
we have is the word & it runs
circles around blockheads like me.

Receipt poem No. 5

It's funny—no smell
does have a kind of smell
but like my olfactory receptors
I opt to bypass its description.
Which has always been
the weakest aspect of my pen.
You can call it work
insomuch that I'm likely
a bad boss to myself.
Or what some dub
a "players' coach."
There's no greater athlete than
Time—
each of us tagged
at the end of the line.
But I like to think of that
fabled runner as
kind enough to wait up for us,
rain or …
What some dub a soft touch.
It's true—you can't make a poem
w/o breaking a few eggs.
Grandpa hated eggs. He was not
a scribe, making my job easier
and unfathomably treacherous.
I've no desire to resurrect the dead
w/ the sorcery of select symbols—
a lie on select nights.
When the writer claimed the Word
saved her, I knew she was a
pufferfish. If the headless
bones of Shakespeare still expect
their audience, why shouldn't
there be those among us who delight
in the indoctrination of poison?

Water-lid poem No. 2

I dreamt my poem
was writing me—she
wouldn't blink like a Brontë
portrait & I couldn't disappear
even w/ eyes closed & redrawn over
my lids—she erased my feet, my
mind—wandering on the road, in the
snow, I imagined the moon
singing, "You know me in dark
only thru the light"—&
I chased her voice   thru the night where we were   everywhere   but lost.

Gum-wrapper poem No. 42

it was easy
2 be an open
book when no
1 read you—
a white rug
when nobody opened
the door—
the small paradise
of swallowing
my words—
dynamite for
dessert.

12/3/22

Brown-napkin poem No. 24

There's no end to a project like
this—to an exercise in the light like
self-awareness in the night—a bright
day so nicely lit it chills me to the bone—
whoever's up there, I must be some kinda
fly skating on ice—from my dark long
sleeve I retrieve a strand of auburn hair
buried halfway & I think I ought to've
left it untouched like so many unturned
                              leaves
grinded under my feet—I have, oh
yes I do, Lord, the kiss of life
tingling like peppermint dying on my lips
& with continued good luck—for what
else to label it in good faith?—maybe
I'll circle back to this 10-minute effort
reminding me, praying with me:
everything was alright, man. & it was real.
Now throw this shit away & begin again.

12/17/22

Gum-wrapper poem No. 43

The danger of seeing to believe. The
danger of the invisible class. The danger
of Medusa behind our eyes. The danger of
the warm bed. The danger of mahogany
messiahs. The danger of the welcome
mat. The danger of imitation. The danger
of the bird's song. The danger of the spider
on the tongue. The danger of bad tomb
stone poems. The danger of names all wrong.

White-napkin poem No. 26

I wanted to sit at the very edge of my
chair & report like a clairvoyant
the true skeleton veiled by the horizon
but the biting haze of my coffee gives
way to a murkier berth—that I
glow only in your embrace on the scant
mornings-after we share like two chess pieces
holding the line long after the last battle
cry has evaporated in the maw of some
opaque maker or other—wasn't it just
dusk, lover? Wasn't the grime of young
Patti Smith's vinyled vocals the shot of life
most divine, as if the sky brightened in your
eyes? Pushed to the edge again—sunk & Blind.

Brown-napkin poem No. 25

35 degrees. Somewhere in the American Southwest.
Seemed to the poet, writing on a napkin, that our lives—
the lived ones, the ones cut short—amounted to
one unanswerable question. (More than fair, the
frigid air.) He sat fleshing from limb to soul
a character who'd wield an antique sword
in her own backyard when a man in a
North Face jacket w/ coffee in hand approached
him & inquired about the spilled contents of his
pen. Also: the books by his side (by Wanda Coleman
& Denis Johnson). "You get paid for your work?"
asked he, to which the other replied, "You
offering me an honorarium?" The man said,
"Nice shoes—have a kickin' day," & like that
there was hardly room for anything else—not his
10-year-old Air Force Ones, not the stable stage of a
table setting this poem, not the kiss of life on his lips,
not the cashless wallet resting by his hip. A lifetime
of religion hadn't prepared him for this—not quite, not
precisely. For who will undo all the bad words? (This question
shouldn't concern the rad poet.) In due time, the slate
will be swiped clean—the napkin will whimper in the
dustbin of history, & she who wielded the sword will
take w/ her to the grave a mystery unknowable to even
she—all outside my own backyard! In my own
lifetime. How the trees in the city are like small
green explosions & they are in this together. (Mostly?)
How they grow for us in this besainted & quartered
body politic so-called safe from the trappings of darkness
b4 Adam's kind. The long line spread thin like a malnourished
platoon lost in the roots of some untranslated masterplan.
To follow the sunset & hope for peace is a mad dash fast pass for
pistol clash & blood rehash.
The poet's out of steam & space. He was interrupted again, but for reasons boiled down
to "brain projectory," he put the man down, gently. For now.

Brown-napkin poem No. 26

"Sometimes
Reality is the strangest
Fantasy of all"—
So much animation in
That selfie
Which isn't my self
Happening to me, now—
The premonition of backlit
One-way roads on Christmas Day
W/ the saints woven into the
Cloudless blue—that blue,
O God, looking down on us—
If today is a battle
Then viva the Revolution—
Such wisdom in youth—
Peace in pieces in years counted on
Fingers toying w/ the voice of a dream.

12/25/22

Envelope poem

To carry one heart, one tongue, one
Mind, two feet & two hands w/ which to
Carry a loan balance of $22,000. (And then
There's the other one …) The nightmare, the so-called
Dark Horse of the Dream, is the shortest possible distance
To my life—& therefore my vessel of demise. Spooky. On
A lighter note, I haven't
Cursed at any YouTube ads
Today. But now that I mention it …
First-World problems. Baby, the lowest
Common denominator is … the hug.
Don't forget that you're not the name on the
Envelope.

12/26/22

Leaf poem

This is not a leaf.
This isn't trash. I'll be
Brief: This can't last.
The hunter is a lonely heart.
The heart's back is
Always turned.

12/29/22

Gift-card sleeves poem

Korean pagoda & red oaks,
turtles lining the pond's edge w/
sun-craned necks like cypress stumps,
Aldo Leopold's prose in our ears—
thus began our new years, Love—
the treaded trail of conservation,
labyrinthine—67 degrees, post-freeze,
SATX. Napkins & coffee sleeves have
suffered mightily on my watch. (All
trash poetry is trash talk.) Stop—
whosoever said to end not w/ a bang
but a whimper—agreed—but we're
basically idiots. 4-5 books at any
given time in my knapsack. At any
given time, my spine be like: "Seriously,
jackass?" Half the time the answer's
always "yes." Many moons ago my
moon was already Christ's moon &
so too Pilate's   moon. In
other words, my moon was my
mother's, first. & yours first,
too. To think the africanized
bee almost stung you. Then me.
The bloated world less than a
period among many stars from afar.
& w/o you: almost nothing any
more. Or something else entirely.
& I realize: writing to you
is like never dying. Writing
is bleeding & never dying.
That's why I carry more reading
than I can chew. That's why
I take this gift & give it back
to you. God help me.
Trapped & freed.

1/1/23

Business-card poem

I dreamt I was behind me, watching me, the
back of me, a younger me,
a thinner me, a stricter me, cheap haircut,
and he was carrying a
gym bag, one I've never owned, and a book
under his arm, *The*
Pillow Book by Sei Shōnagan, over 1,000 years
old, a book I've
only slept on, and I followed this young man
who played it safe,
who didn't own the fear to think to look
back, I tailed
this invincible dreamer into a building
and down a
wide hallway until he stopped, dropped
the bag,
knelt & retrieved from it what
seemed a
small leather Bible, no, it was a
pistol, a
revolver, he was aiming it at
me,
I knew he was capable of it, I
would've done the same thing, we won the
game.

White-napkin poem No. 27

White hair on my beard inching
toward Babylon—
I never met a heart I
could call mine—
Last night I said, "Look at the moon"
and the world of color fled
on its head—there is something
happening—the language under my
skin / not mine—what comes
after poetry / white noise
spilled on the napkin spilled
on the liquid drop
asking for nothing like
The Void—I never had a heart
I couldn't destroy—the hereafter
design of bipedal desire spilled
on The Void spilled on the other
wise silent napkin—I never met
a line I couldn't destroy—
I wore the sky on my sleeve
hoping you'd see—I went to
sleep with bright visions & there
was Death to greet me on the mountain
retreat—the look of recognition / the sun
under my
suite.

1/10/23

White-napkin poem No. 28

Up 1604 & the panzers of intelligence
Around me the whipping speed
Why nobody's come at me with
"Harmony's nickname can only be
Harm"
Is because they're wise not to lend literature
Lines the foolish streetwise panthers of
Intelligence surrounding everywhere the
Whipping harmony of mornings splashed down
Caromed chrome crossings God why has
Nobody told me how it'd be
Is that a gasoline tank or lunchbox in her
Hands is she still loved from the ground up
Well hell—she's crying laughing.

1/12/23

AARP Bulletin poem

I sit here at
the edge of a
papercut
pen in
hand
like a
friend
but not
like the
sunlight
leaked
on
me
in
bands
like
a complicated
secret
alone &
used like
the pen in
my hand
not a friend
but
a lover
w/ no
agenda
or body
like mine
far away
even from me
pockets empty
like words lost in the fog of your touch.

1/16/23

Chopstick poem

Lately on walks I've let my old head inside the sacred shrine. Mess-talk. SMACK! went the playpen palm. Company dime.

Gum-wrapper poem No. 44

Watched the clock waggle
round my crown. Had
the time for those who
ran w/ mine. Only
odd ducks get even w/ trash. It's
Liberation
Night!

1/17/23

Plastic-knife poem

Dark marks on the chopping block
Atop the right lap, my word!
What's more agreeable than that?

1/20/23

Receipt poem No. 6

A year & a half like a thousand
thunderstorms washing your sad grass eyes—
I want to write for tomorrow's ghost children
but like Saturn's rings every loose poem
shed for you—don't believe the
words which kept you like your favorite romance
lost in the fire of new silence.

1/23/23

ABOUT THE AUTHOR

Alex Z. Salinas is the author of four poetry collections and a book of stories, *City Lights From the Upside Down*, which was included in the National Book Critics Circle's Critical Notes. He holds an M.A. in English Literature and Language from St. Mary's University, and lives in San Antonio, Texas.

ABOUT THE PHOTOGRAPHER

Margaret Cavazos is an aspiring renaissance (wo)man. She enjoys traveling, camping, hiking, history podcasts, anime and sunrises. She is a graduate of St. Mary's University where she studied history and criminal justice.

www.ingramcontent.com/pod-product-compliance
Lightning Source LLC
Chambersburg PA
CBHW041534120626
46551CB00019B/2694